FUNCTIONAL SKILLS:

ENGLISH
LEVEL 2

Roslyn Whitley Willis

Published by
Lexden Publishing Ltd
www.lexden-publishing.co.uk

About the Author

Roslyn Whitley Willis has worked as a Key Skills tutor, assessor, verifier and co-ordinator in further and higher education. Additionally she has worked independently as a Key Skills consultant. She is the author of 16 widely accepted Key Skills text books.

Roslyn has incorporated, and extended, the principles that were successful in her Key Skills text books and sees as key to helping centres make the transition from Key Skills to Functional Skills and students gain the qualification.

To ensure that your book is up to date visit:
www.lexden-publishing.co.uk/functionalskills/update.htm

Acknowledgements

My thanks go to my husband and friends who have been tolerant of my absences during the writing of this book. A special mention for Jean, my chosen sister.
– *Roslyn Whitley Willis.*

First Published in 2008 by Lexden Publishing Ltd.

British Library Cataloguing in Publication Data.

A CIP record of this book is available from the British Library

ISBN 978-1-904995-50-0

Typeset and designed by Lexden Publishing Ltd.

Printed by Lightning Source.

Lexden Publishing Ltd
Email: info@lexden-publishing.co.uk
www.lexden-publishing.co.uk

CONTENTS

FUNCTIONAL SKILLS: ENGLISH LEVEL 2

INTRODUCTION

The purpose of Functional Skills English is to provide a qualification that will prepare you, the learner, for the skills you will need in work, for progressing through education and in your everyday life.

Having these skills will help the individual person and the employee to work confidently, effectively and independently.

The skills which are important include being able to:

- read and understand information of various types, such as instructions; timetables; graphs and charts; letters from organisations; newspaper articles; maps; and information located on the world wide web;
- read and understand documents on a range of subjects both familiar and unfamiliar to you;
- show an understanding of information you find and write a range of documents that summarise the information;
- write a range of documents such as those required in business – letters, memos and reports - and those needed in personal life, such as letters and instructions;
- write documents that are suited to the reader and the subject;
- write documents that convey the information and your meaning clearly, and that use correct English grammar, punctuation and spelling;
- listen to group and one to one discussions and show an understanding of what is being said by others;
- speak in groups, and to groups, exchange ideas and opinions and express your ideas so the listeners can follow what you say.

The material in this book gives you the opportunity to acquire, and apply, this knowledge and these skills.

This book is in three sections.

Section 1 gives guidance on some aspects of English grammar to help your writing skills, and some guidance on words to avoid when involved in discussions.

Section 2 provides Reference Sheets that cover the background information to prepare you for the activities that follow in Section 3. These Reference Sheets aid your learning and understanding, and can be used for revision.

Section 3 is made up of practice tasks covering a range of employment sectors. These tasks are designed to help you produce work at the correct level and also help you become confident, competent and prepared for the assessment of Functional English Level 2. The assessment will test your ability to apply what you have learnt in the subject to everyday contexts which are not linked to specific employment sectors.

SECTION 1

BRUSH UP YOUR WRITING AND SPEAKING SKILLS

Apostrophes

Using apostrophes correctly is easy. Just follow these rules.

The two main reasons for using apostrophes are:

1   to show a letter, or letters, are omitted in a word; and

2   to show possession.

Rule 1 — to show where a letter (or letters) has been missed out

don't	means	do not	the apostrophe is placed where the letter "o" has been left out.
I don't (do n[o]t) know where the hotel is located.			

didn't	means	did not	the apostrophe is placed where the letter "o" has been left out.
I didn't (did n[o]t) go to college yesterday.			

I'm	means	I am	the apostrophe is placed where the letter "a" has been left out.
I'm (I [a]m) going to the party on Saturday.			
I do not feel as if I'm (I [a]m) able to visit him.			

she'll	means	she will	the apostrophe is placed where the letters "w" and "i" have been left out.
She'll (she [wi]ll) come to the wedding next month.			

haven't	means	have not	the apostrophe is placed where the letter "o" has been left out.
I haven't (have n[o]t) got an examination date yet.			

4

it's	means	it is	the apostrophe is placed where the letter "i" has been left out.

It's (it [i]s) easy to get to her home.

It's (it [i]s) not difficult to pass the test.

we're	means	we are	the apostrophe is placed where the letter "a" has been left out.

We're (we [a]re) all going to the fair in February.

I am not sure we're (we [a]re) entered for the examination.

they'll	means	they will	the apostrophe is placed where the letters "w" and "i" have been left out.

They'll (they [wi]ll) decide whether to live in Australia.

who's	means	who is	the apostrophe is placed where the letter "i" has been left out.

Who's (who [i]s) the best driver?

you're	means	you are	the apostrophe is placed where the letter "a" has been left out.

You're (you [a]re) not taking this seriously.

I am not sure you're (you [a]re) going to pass.

Exercise

Try to put the correct word using the apostrophe in the following sentences. (Be careful! There are some which are not in the previous examples, so you will have to think about them!)

1   (We are) _____ bringing father home from hospital next Monday.

2   (It is) _____ so easy to do this exercise.

3   (They are) _____ going to Budapest for their holiday this year.

4   It (is not) _____ his car which was stolen.

5   He is not sure (I am) _____ invited to the fair.

6   (It is) _____ easy for you to say that, but I (have not) _____ got a clue.

7   (What is) _____ the matter with your car, Harry?

8   (It is) _____ the exhaust, and (they are) _____ not sure they can put it right.

9   (You are) _____ going to have to hire a car (are not) _____ you?

10   Yes, (it will) _____ be an expensive few days when (I have) _____ not got my car.

Rule 2 — To show someone, or something, possesses (owns) something

Singular Words

In the English language we do not say things like ....

collar of the cat	(singular — one cat)
hat of the boy	(singular — one boy)
shoes of the lady	(singular — one lady)
legs of the chair	(singular — one chair)
house of the mother	(singular — one mother)

Instead we structure sentences which indicate someone, or something, possesses (owns) something by using an apostrophe.

The order of the words in the sentences that require apostrophes is this:

<table>
<tr><td align="center">**1st**</td><td align="center">**2nd**</td></tr>
<tr><td align="center">**who** or **what** does the owning</td><td align="center">**what** is owned</td></tr>
</table>

For example:

In the phrase '**collar of the cat**' ask yourself — **who owns what**?

Answer: one cat owns the collar.

So the order is '**cat**' then '**collar**'.

In the phrase '**house of the mother**' ask yourself — **who owns what**?

Answer: one mother owns the house.

So the order is '**mother**' then '**house**'.

Where do I put in the Apostrophe?

!!!! Don't worry — It's easy !!!!

Follow these five simple steps

Step 1: write down the word which represents the person or thing doing the owning.

cat

Step 2: next to that write what is owned.

cat collar

Step 3: think once more about who or what does the owning, in this case **cat**, and <u>underline</u> it.

<u>cat</u> collar

Step 4: next put the apostrophe **after** the <u>underlined</u> word.

<u>cat</u>' collar

Step 5: finally, as the word **cat** is singular, add a letter **s** <u>after</u> the apostrophe.

<u>cat</u>'s collar

Let's try it with "house of the mother".

Step 1: write down the word which represents the person or thing doing the owning.

mother

Step 2: next write what is owned.

mother house

Step 3: think once more about who or what does the owning, in this case **mother**, and <u>underline</u> it.

<u>mother</u> house

Step 4: next put the apostrophe **after** the <u>underlined</u> word.

<u>mother</u>' house

Step 5: finally, as the word **mother** is singular, add a letter **s** after the apostrophe.

<u>mother</u>'s house

Let's try it with "shoes of the lady".

Step 1: write down the word which represents the person or thing doing the owning.

lady

Step 2: next write what is owned.

lady **shoes**

Step 3: think once more about who or what does the owning, in this case **lady**, and <u>underline</u> it.

<u>lady</u> shoes

Step 4: next put the apostrophe **after** the <u>underlined</u> word.

<u>lady</u>' shoes

Step 5: finally, as the word **lady** is singular, add a letter **s** after the apostrophe.

<u>lady</u>'s shoes

To Summarise

1   Decide **who or what** owns.

2   Write down that word.

3   **Underline** that word.

4   Put the apostrophe **after** the underlined word.

5   If the word is **singular** add an 's' **after** the apostrophe.

Exercise

Put in the apostrophe for each of the following, singular, owners:

1   the boy owning the hat _____

2   the chair owning the legs_____

3   the man owning the briefcase _____

4   the dog owning the bone _____

5   the student owning the pen _____

Rule 2 – To show a group of people, or things, possess (own) something

Plural words (ending in the letter s)

Examples:

      ladies owning club   (many ladies)

      boys owning football   (many boys)

      dogs owning collars   (many dogs)

In the phrase '**ladies owning club**' ask yourself **who owns what?**

      Answer: the ladies (plural) own a club.

So the order is '**ladies**' then '**club**'.

Where do I put in the apostrophe?

!!!! Good news – there are only four steps in this one !!!

Step 1: write down the word that represents the people or things doing the owning.

ladies

Step 2: next write what is owned.

ladies club (many ladies owning a club)

Step 3: think once more about who or what does the owning, in this case **ladies**, and <u>underline</u> it.

<u>ladies</u> club

Step 4: **finally** put the apostrophe **after** the <u>underlined</u> word.

<u>ladies</u>' club

There's no need to put a letter **s** after the word <u>ladies</u> as it ends in a letter s.

Let's try it with boys owning a football.

Step 1: write down the word that represents the people or things doing the owning.

boys

Step 2: next write what is owned.

boys football (one football owned by many boys)

Step 3: think once more about who or what does the owning, in this case **boys**, and <u>underline</u> it.

<u>boys</u> football

Step 4: **finally** put the apostrophe **after** the <u>underlined</u> word.

<u>boys</u>' football

There's no need to put a letter s after the word <u>boys</u> as it ends in a letter **s**.

Let's try it with dogs owning collars.

Step 1: write down the word which represents the people or things doing the owning.

dogs

Step 2: next write what is owned.

<big>dogs collars</big> (many dogs owning many collars)

Step 3: think once more about who or what does the owning, in this case **dogs**, and <u>underline</u> it.

<big><u>**dogs**</u> collars</big>

Step 4: **finally** put the apostrophe **after** the <u>underlined</u> word.

<big><u>**dogs**</u>' collars</big>

There's no need to put a letter **s** after the word <u>dogs</u> as it ends in a letter **s**.

> **NOTE: There's no need to put an apostrophe in collars because it's just a plural word – it doesn't own anything and there's no letter omitted.**

To Summarise

1   Decide **who or what** owns.

2   Write down that word.

3   **Underline** that word.

4   Put the apostrophe **after** the underlined word.

Exercise

Put in the apostrophe for each of the following, plural, owners.

Remember: it's only the people or things doing the owning that need an apostrophe.

1   the clubs owning the football ground _____

2   the students owning the text books _____

3   the tutors owning the pens _____

4   the cars owning the exhausts _____

5   the boxers owning competitions _____

One Extra Rule About Apostrophes

You have learnt that whatever or whoever does the owning has the apostrophe somewhere.

You know how to work out that "somewhere" – write the word down, underline it, then put the apostrophe **after** the word.

So you have: man's son; ladies' meeting; students' calculator; dogs' bones

But

When the thing/person that owns is already plural — children, men, women - then you must put the apostrophe after that word, as usual, **then put on the letter 's'.**

For example: the <u>men</u>'s club   (one club owned by many men)

                 the <u>children</u>'s toys   (many children owning many toys)

                 the <u>women</u>'s clothes   (the clothes owned by many women).

You are still thinking about who or what does the owning, putting the apostrophe after it, then adding an s.

There's an exception, but don't worry about it.

You will have possibly seen a reference to a Charles Dickens's book, or Tom Jones's singing career? My name is Willis, so you would be quite correct in writing "Roslyn

Willis's book". This is not wrong, but this does look messy and therefore it's quite acceptable when names end in the letter **s** to just put the apostrophe after the **s**. It's so much nicer to read Roslyn Willis' book, and Tom Jones' voice.

So, when the word ends in s put the apostrophe after it and STOP.

Exercise

Put in the apostrophe for each of the following. Think carefully about the word that represents who, or what, is doing the owning, and if it is plural or singular.

1   The children owning a playground _____

2   The school owning the piano _____

3   The piano owning the keys _____

4   The cats owning the whiskers _____

5   The gentlemen owning a club _____

6   The policemen owning uniforms _____

7   The student owning a computer _____

8   The man owning a car _____

9   The car owning a steering wheel _____

10   The employee owning a desk _____

I Before E - Except After C

Sometimes it is necessary to learn some spelling rules to help you get your work correct. The "i" before "e" rule is one of them.

It's an easy rule: use i **before e, except after c.**

Which means that you will **usually** use **ie** in such words as:

believe; sieve; grieve.

But you will use **ei** when the **e** follows the letter **c** in such words as:

receive; receipt; perceive.

There are some exceptions such as **weird and weight** but that's all the more reason to use your dictionary.

Exercise

Choose the word that is spelt correctly in each of the following sentences. **Then find each word in the grid in the next exercise.**

1   I must achieve/acheive better examination results this year.

2   It is easy to believe/beleive he is the best student.

3   The ceiling/cieling of our kitchen needs to be painted.

4   A train that carries goods, not passengers, is called a frieght/freight train.

5   We get on very well with our neighbours/nieghbours.

6   I offered her a peice/piece of cake but she refused it.

7   Our local priest/preist is retiring next year.

8   When you buy goods you should always keep the receipt/reciept in case you need to return the goods to the shop.

9   Queen Victoria is said to have had the longest reign/riegn in the United Kingdom.

10   It was a releif/relief to see him looking so well after his operation.

11   At Christmas it is common to hear the sleigh/sliegh bells in the clear, quiet night.

12   I donated blood the other day. It involved putting a needle into my veins/viens.

13   Please weigh/wiegh the butter carefully. If you get it wrong, the cake will be ruined.

14   This year the farmers say their crops have a greater yeild/yield than last year.

Now use your answers to find the words in the word search in the next exercise.

Exercise

Now find the words you found in the previous exercise word search in this word search.

```
M A L M H E O S D F G Q O R A
U K O Z F P B T N W L X D C E
R E L I E F H G I E W D H G V
U T E P V I M O N E T I N H E
S R U O B H G I E N E I G V I
T P R T Z S B A A V L I S V L
X S I H P I S J E I E T E D E
S L E E D I X V E L H I L G B
L C H I C E E C S G N E L E A
L J I X R E Y C I S I U R G W
A C Z C Q P Q E E Y M J J X N
C E Y M D L R E S R Z V S K D
U V I U V F U N G I E R H R X
S I F T D Q X X D H Z T M U H
V J Z L K U K E I C S Z A R F
```

There, Their and They're

There house is in Carlisle. Their very proud of it because they have spent the last three years doing some rebuilding and lots of decorating without any help from they're family or there friends.

Can you spot the words which are used incorrectly in the above sentences?

No? It all looks right?

These words look and sound similar and sometimes it can be difficult to decide how to use *there*, *their* and *they're* correctly.

Read the information in each of the examples, test yourself, then go back to those sentences and you should be able to correct them with ease.

There

This indicates a location, so when you use this word you might be talking about a direction.

Examples using "there":

>   **There** are the crayons I thought I had lost.
>
>   My house is over **there**.
>
>   **Tip** It is a place word so it has the word **here** in it. (*See page 24.*)

Their

This word indicates that more than one person, or thing, possesses something.

Examples using "their":

>   Ask them if they want to book **their** holiday yet.
>
>   It is always easy to see **their** point of view.
>
>   **Tip:** As this word can relate to people think "her" and "him" (e and i) — their.

They're

Because this word has an apostrophe in it, it is an indication that something has been left out. In this case it is the letter "a". (*See page 4 and 5, Apostrophes.*)

This word means they (a)re.

Examples using "they're":

> **They're** going to buy a new car next year.
>
> I cannot contact Paul and Roisin as **they're** out of the office today.

Exercise

Try to put the correct their, there or they're in the following sentences:

1   I'm going _____ tomorrow.

2   It's possible to get _____ by train but it is easier to go by bus.

3   _____ grandmother has a large house in Suffolk and _____ going for two weeks in the spring.

4   Perhaps _____ should be some rules about using the photocopier.

5   _____ going to _____ cousin's wedding next Saturday. Will you also be _____?

6   _____ on a cruise in the Indian Ocean until the 17th.

7   We had a postcard which they posted in the Seychelles. _____ having a good time it seems.

8   Tomorrow _____ ship is due back into Southampton.

9   _____ are quite a few people going to _____ party on Wednesday.

10   _____ Uncle is over in Prague. Have you been _____?

Now go back to the sentences at the top of *page 17* and find the errors. It should be easy now.

To, Two and Too

We have to many problems at work, which means we are not able two concentrate on sending out the orders too the clients. Can you suggest the best way too solve these problems?

Can you spot the words which are used incorrectly in the above sentences?

No? It all looks right?

These words look similar and they all sound the same so sometimes it can be difficult to decide how to use *to, two* and *too* correctly.

Read the information for each of the examples, test yourself, then go back to those sentences and you should be able to correct them with ease.

To

This is known as a **preposition** and is a word that indicates direction. A preposition is a word which is used to join words and create phrases, usually related to time or place.

Examples of prepositions:

The cat sat **on** the mat.

She comes **from** Manchester.

The house is **by** the sea.

The weather **in** Spain is hot.

The water runs **under** the bridge.

I will be there **by** 11am.

Examples using "to":

They are going **to** the restaurant.

It is easy **to** swim in the ocean.

Two

Two is the written form of the number "2".

> **Examples using "two":**
>
> The recipe uses **two** ounces of flour.
>
> There are **two** hundred bulbs in the garden.

Too

Too means "also" , "as well" and "very".

> **Examples using "too":**
>
> Harriet said she was hungry, then Flavia said she was hungry **too** (also/as well).
>
> Niall wanted an ice-cream **too** (also/as well).
>
> His car is just too (very) big.
>
> The children's behaviour was **too** (very) mischievous.

Exercise

Try to put the correct to, too or two in the following sentences:

1	I really am _____ tired to continue with this now.

2	It's possible to get _____ involved in the game.

3	There are _____ excellent teams in the final.

4	John and Meena are going _____ Southampton to meet their grandparents tomorrow.

5	If you are going _____ the shops, please bring me back _____ loaves of bread.

6	We have _____ much work to do and cannot go _____ the disco.

7	It's always difficult _____ think about saving, but the _____ of us need to save for our holiday next year.

8	We have _____ many problems at the moment.

9	We need _____ get at least 70% in order _____ pass this examination.

10	It would seem that there are _____ guests _____ many at the party.

Now go back to the sentences at the top of *page 19* and find the errors. It should be easy now.

Where, Were and We're

Were going to the wedding of Paul and Molly but where not sure we're the church is located. Our grandparents where coming with us but now were going alone.

Can you spot the words which are used incorrectly in the above sentences?

No? It all looks right?

Because these words look similar it can be difficult to decide how to use *where*, *were* and *we're* correctly.

Read the information in each of the examples, test yourself, then go back to those sentences and you should be able to correct them with ease.

Where

This indicates a location.

Examples using "where":

> Where are they going for their holiday this year?

> I do not know where I am going.

Tip: Where is a place word so it has the word **here** in it. (*See page 24.*)

Were

This word indicates something happened in the past.

Examples using "were":

> They were almost home when the car broke down.

> We were going to Haslam's Mini Mart, but someone said it was closed.

We're

This word means we (a)re.

Because this word has an apostrophe in it, it is an indication that something has been left out. In this case it is the letter "a". (*See page 5, Apostrophes.*)

Examples using "we're":

> We're going to Harrogate to do some shopping.
>
> Tell us if we're not welcome.

Exercise

Try to put the correct word, where, were or we're in the following sentences:

1   It is easy to see _____ the new building is going to be.

2   _____ are the CDs?

3   There _____ 17 chairs in the room.

4   If _____ going to be at the cinema in time we need to set off now.

5   I could not tell if Janseed and Abrim _____ at the club today.

6   _____ is the nearest health club with a tennis court?

7   Janice is going to Majorca and _____ off to Sardinia next month.

8   I know _____ the nearest car park is.

9   I expect _____ going to have to save a lot more money if we want to buy our own home.

10   Jack and Harriet _____ only staying overnight with their cousins.

Now go back to the sentences at the top of *page 22* and find the errors. It should be easy now.

Here, Hear or Heard?

"Hear you are Solomon. I herd you asking if the magazine was here", said Chris. "I here you are going to get hear by noon. Tell me if I herd correctly", said Issac.

Can you spot the words which are used incorrectly in the above sentences?

No? They look all right?

These words look and sound fairly similar so sometimes it can be difficult to decide how to use here, hear and heard correctly.

Read the information in each of the examples, test yourself, then go back to those sentences and you should be able to correct them with ease.

Here

This word usually relates to a place: **in** a place or **at** a place.

Examples using "here":

> Here are the eggs.
>
> I'm over here.
>
> It's best to look here rather than there.

Did you notice that here appears in the word **"there"**?

Remember both words are about places and directions so the spelling is almost the same.

Hear and Heard

Look at the three letters — **ear**

This should give you a clue about when to use this word.

It's about anything to do with hearing.

Examples using "hear" and "heard":

> I hear you. [Compare this with I heard you. Notice "heard" begins with the word "hear".]
>
> Do you hear me? We must hear what they have to say.

But What About "Herd"?

This sounds the same as the verb "heard", but it is a word used quite differently!

I'm sure you've heard about a herd of cows!

Remember: if it is anything to do with hearing "ear" appears in the word.

Exercise

Try to put the correct word, here, hear or heard in the following sentences:

1   It was _____ last time I saw it.

2   It's possible to _____ the argument but not agree with it.

3   Send them a map to show them the way _____.

4   I work _____ each weekend.

5   On the map mark the turns so they can get _____.

6   Yesterday I _____ the church bells ringing for forty minutes.

7   Did you _____ the thunder last night?

8   Come over _____ please, I cannot _____ what you are saying.

9   If you want to live _____ you will have to make some plans.

10   The move _____ seems to have been a good one I think.

Now go back to the sentences at the top of *page 24* and find the errors. It should be easy now.

Do I Use "Amount" or "Number"?

These two words both refer to quantities, but are used differently according to the **noun** in the sentence. A noun is a word which usually refers to a place or a thing.

> **Examples of nouns:**
>
> The **cat** slept on the **sofa**.
>
> An **egg** should be boiled in a **pan** for four minutes.
>
> The **boy** always comes home with **mud** on his **shoes**.

Amount

Amount is used with singular nouns.

> **Examples:**
>
> **(in each case the singular noun is emboldened)**
>
> The amount of **money** we have to spend each week is decreasing.
>
> I only have a limited amount of **time** I can spend with you today.
>
> You will have to give a certain amount of **thought** to this question.

Number

Number is used with **plural** nouns.

> **Examples:**
>
> **(in each case the plural noun is emboldened)**
>
> The number of **students** has increased this year.
>
> There are a greater number of **people** in the restaurant than usual this evening.
>
> The number of **opportunities** Sidra has had cannot be counted.
>
> The number of **books** on the shelves has increased.

Exercise

Try to put the correct word, "amount" or "number", in the following sentences.

In the first three sentences the **noun** is emboldened to help you.

TIP: Think what "amount" or "number" is describing (look for the noun). If it's singular use *amount*, if it's plural use *number*.

1 The _____ of holiday **destinations** in the brochure means we have plenty of choice.

2 There are a _____ of **jobs** to be done before we can go home today.

3 I was shocked by the _____ of **help** Petri needed with his project.

4 The _____ of clothes in her wardrobe is quite impressive.

5 I only have a small _____ of money to spend on presents for my family.

6 I have to write a project containing a large _____ of pages.

7 You will need a greater _____ of cash if you want to buy that car.

8 The _____ of noise at the concert was very high.

9 I expect there will be a greater _____ of accidents on the roads this year.

10 The _____ of food we will need for the party will increase if you are inviting another six people.

Is it "Less" or "Fewer"?

These two words have similar meanings, but are used differently according to the noun in the sentence.

Less

Less is used with **singular** nouns.

Examples:

(in each case the singular noun is emboldened)

There is less **money** to spend each week.

I have less **opportunity** for leisure time than last year because I am working longer hours.

There is less **noise** in the classroom today.

Fewer

Fewer is used with **plural** nouns.

Examples:

(in each case the plural noun is emboldened)

There are fewer **students** taking this examination this term.

Fewer **people** attended the car rally last Sunday.

No fewer than four **countries** may vote.

Exercise

Try to put the correct word, "less" or "fewer" in the following sentences.

In the first three sentences the **noun** is emboldened to help you.

TIP: Think what "less" or "fewer" is describing (look for the noun). If it's singular use *less*, it it's plural use *fewer*.

1   I need _____ **help** with my work now I am beginning to understand this subject.

2   There are _____ **jobs** to be done in the office today.

3   The building industry has _____ **employees** than this month last year.

4   It took me _____ time to swim the length of the pool today.

5   I will need _____ than a pint of milk for that recipe.

6   Usually in the post office on Tuesdays there are _____ people in the queue.

7   There are _____ colleges offering language courses this year.

8   I have _____ money than I had last month because I bought a new iPod.

9   Jamil has _____ relatives than Marshall.

10 There are _____ holiday destinations in the brochure and this limits our choice.

Do I Use "Accept" or "Except"?

These two words can cause confusion as they look similar and can sound similar, but they have very different meanings so it is important that you remember the difference.

Accept

Accept means to admit, to agree, to put up with, to take on.

Accept is a verb — a "doing word" — a word where the word "to" can be put in front of it.

Examples of verbs:

To fly　　　To murmur　　To leap　　　To learn　　　To accept

Examples using "accept":

I **accept** you are the better driver. (admit/agree)

I gratefully **accept** the present you have sent me. (take on)

You will just have to **accept** that the working conditions are not ideal. (put up with the fact that)

Will he **accept** my offer of help do you think? (agree to)

Except

Except usually means something, or someone, is left out or excluded.

Examples using "except":

We all went to the bar, **except** Tony who was not feeling very well.

I remembered to pack the shoes I would need on holiday, all **except** the black ones.

Mother put the cakes in an oven which was too hot. She managed to save all of them **except** one.

Exercise

Try to put the correct word, "accept" or "except" in the following sentences:

1   I am not able to _____ your advice because I don't agree
     with it.

2   He will just have to _____ that I am right on this occasion.

3   Invite everyone from the year group _____ Molly who will be on
     holiday.

4   Molly is not able to _____ our invitation as she will be on
     holiday.

5   I would ask Naomi to lend me her car _____ that I know
     it's in the garage being repaired.

6   I hope the University will _____ me onto the course?

7   I cannot _____ your gift; it is far too expensive.

8   You don't need to bring anything _____ yourself!

9   Just _____ you have lost the bet.

10   The supermarket had everything I wanted _____ the eggs.

Is It "Advise" or "Advice"?

These two words have a very similar meaning as they're both to do with giving and receiving information. Which word has to be used depends upon whether you are receiving information or giving it.

Advise

To advise means to tell or inform someone of something.

Advise is a verb — a "**doing** word" — a word where the word "to" can be put in front of it.

Examples of verbs:

To swim   To hear   To think   To pounce   To advise

Examples using "advise" and "advised":

I advised him the tyres on his car were flat.

She advised me about how to complete my application form.

I will advise my friend about the best driving school to go to for lessons.

It is easy to advise him; he always listens.

In all these examples someone is **doing** something.

Advice

Advice is some**thing** you give to someone, usually as a result of them asking for your ideas and opinions. (Whether they take your advice is a different matter!!)

Advice is a noun – a word which has in front of it a definite, or indefinite, article.

Examples of definite and indefinite articles:

Definite article	Indefinite article
The computer	An egg
The home	An atmosphere
	A home
	A field

Examples using advice:

The **advice** I will give you is not to buy that car.

Any **advice** I give you I know you will ignore.

The best **advice** I have to offer is to book your holiday early.

In all these examples some**thing** is being given.

TIP: use "c" for nouns
use "s" for verbs

Exercise

Try to put the correct word, advise or advice, in the following sentences. Think about whether something is being given or received, and if you are using a noun or a verb.

1   Please _____ me of your new address.

2   I do not want _____ on a subject you know nothing about.

3   I will be here to _____ you if you wish.

4   I never offer _____ to anybody.

5   Ask Naomi for _____; she is the best person to help you.

6   Shall I ask _____ from Darren?

7   I wonder where I can get _____ about moving to Scotland.

8   I always go to Barbara when I want _____.

9   What would you _____ him to do?

10   It's easy to give _____ but not so easy to take it.

Is it "Practise" or "Practice"?

These two words look very similar, they sound the same, which is why there is so much confusion in choosing which to use, but there is a definite difference in their meanings.

Practise

To practise means to **carry out** or **do**. It is often something you **do** repeatedly to get better at doing something, for example football skills or dance moves.

Practise is a verb — a "doing word" — a word where the word "to" can be put in front of it.

Examples of verbs:

To run   To thank   To surf   To jump   To practise

Examples using practise:

I practised my French verbs for two hours.

She practised her freestyle stroke.

I have to practise my yoga every day.

In all these examples someone is **doing** something.

Practice

Practice relates to some**thing**.

Practice is a noun — a word which has in front of it a definite, or indefinite, article.

Examples of nouns with definite and indefinite articles:

Definite Article	**Indefinite article**
The dental practice	A practice manager
The practice building	A practice lap

Examples using practice:

> The practice of buying fresh vegetables daily is a healthy one.
>
> It is a good practice to recycle as much as possible.
>
> In both these examples some**thing** is being described.

> **TIP:** use "c" for nouns
> use "s" for verbs

Exercise

Try to put the correct word, practise or practice, in the following sentences. Think if the word is a verb (practise) or a noun (practice).

1   Please _____ your golf swing.

2   You need to _____ your singing if you want to join our choir.

3   The _____ manager is on holiday next week.

4   My dental _____ is closed all day Thursday.

5   Only _____ can help you do something better.

6   It's hard to _____ daily as I am tired after work.

7   I wonder where I can _____ my drumming without disturbing anyone?

8   I always go out when Bob begins his _____.

9   What would you like to _____ today?

10   I don't agree with the _____ of fox hunting.

Do I Have an "Affect" or an "Effect"?

These two words look and sound similar, but have different meanings.

Affect

Affect means to change, or have an influence upon.

Affect is a verb — a "doing word" — a word where the word "to" can be put in front of it.

Examples of verbs:

To learn	To mime	To shriek	To drive	To affect

Examples using affect:

Will the exercise **affect** my fitness? (change/influence)

How will global warming **affect** the world climate? (influence)

The new law will not **affect** your business. (change)

Effect

Effect means the result of something, a consequence of something happening. (What will happen if ....)

Effect is a noun — a word which has in front of it a definite, or indefinite, article.

Examples of nouns with definite and indefinite articles:

Definite article	Indefinite article
The holiday	An opinion
The park	An orange
	A customer
	A tent

Examples using effect:

Exercise must have an **effect** on my fitness because I can climb 100 steps without stopping now that I am exercising regularly. (The **result** of exercise has made me fitter.)

The effect of global warming is likely to be a change in the climate of the world. (A consequence of global warming is a change in world climate.)

The effect (result) of this new law upon my business is that it will cost more to pay my employees.

Exercise

Try to put the correct word, affect or effect, in the following sentences:

1   How will that law _____ me?

2   Will the exchange rate _____ how much money you take on holiday?

3   When your brother emigrates to Canada, how will this _____ your family?

4   If I don't send out the invitations to the wedding in time, what _____ will that have on the caterers?

5   If I recycle more in the office, what _____ will that have for the planet?

6   Do you really think that will _____ me?

7   How does the reduction in the speed limit _____ your journey to Manchester?

8   What is the _____ of losing sleep?

9   How will losing sleep _____ me?

10   The supermarket put up its price of fish and that had an _____ upon what I chose to cook for dinner.

To "Borrow" or to "Lend"?

These two words are very different, yet there is some confusion as to which should be used. Remember this, you can't borrow something unless it has been lent to you!

Borrow

Borrow = from

Borrow relates to something you have temporarily **from** someone.

Borrowed is the past tense of the verb to "borrow".

> **Examples using borrow and borrowed:**
>
> I will **borrow** the book **from** Harry.
>
> Harry **borrowed** the book **from** me.
>
> "May I **borrow** your pen, please?"

Lend

Lend = to

Lend is something you temporarily give **to** someone.

Lent is the past tense of the verb to "lend".

> **Examples using lend and lent:**
>
> I will **lend** the book **to Benny**.
>
> Benny **lent** the book **to** me.
>
> "Would you **lend** me your pen, please?"

Exercise

Try to put the correct word, borrow(ed), lent or lend(s), in the following sentences:

1   Ask Mr Jones next door if I can _____ his ladder.

2   If Mr Jones _____ me his ladder I can repair my roof.

3   Remember if you _____ something, always give it back.

4   "I am sorry, I cannot _____ you my car."

5   I was asked to _____ him my mobile phone, but I refused.

6   "May I _____ your mobile phone please?"

7   If I was to _____ you money, I know you would ask again and again.

8   I _____ my father's car to meet mother from the
     station.

9   Geoff could _____ Keith his motorbike, but he is not going to.

10   "Just don't ask to _____ anything else; you never give it back."

"Able" or "Ible"?

These are suffixes that mean the same thing, i.e. that may be done. For example, visible means may be seen, or laughable which means may be laughed at.

...... able

...... able is a **suffix** (something added to the end of a word).

You would **normally** add **able** if the original (root) word is a word on its own.

> ### Examples adding able:
>
> *laugh* is a word on its own so you would add the suffix **able** to make:
>
> *laughable*
>
> *suit* is a word on its own so you would add the suffix **able** to make:
>
> *suitable*
>
> *depend* is a word on its own so you would add the suffix **able** to make:
>
> *dependable*

...... ible

.... ible is a **suffix**.

You would normally add **ible** if the original (root) word is **not** a word on its own.

> ### Examples adding ible:
>
> *visible* — in this case *vis* is **not** a word on its own so you would add the suffix **ible** to make:
>
> *visible*
>
> *edible* — in this case *ed* is **not** a word on its own so you would add the suffix **ible** to make:
>
> *edible*
>
> *permissible* — in this case *permiss* is **not** a word on its own so you would add the suffix **ible** to make:
>
> *permissible*

What do you do when the original word ends in the letter **e**?

It is **usual** when the root words ends in the letter **e**, to drop the **e** and add the suffix.

Examples of words where the letter e has to be dropped:

advise	becomes	advisable
value	becomes	valuable
desire	becomes	desirable
debate	becomes	debatable

Remember, the English language has exceptions to rules (times when the "normal" rules don't apply). If in doubt and when faced with an unfamiliar word –

USE YOUR DICTIONARY.

Exercise: Am I Able.............?

Decide which word of the following pairs is spelt correctly. Place a tick ✓ next to the correctly spelt word, **then find that word in the grid below:**

comfortable	☐	comfortible	☐
fashionable	☐	fashionible	☐
incredible	☐	incredable	☐
laughible	☐	laughable	☐
possible	☐	possable	☐
suitable	☐	suitible	☐
terrable	☐	terrible	☐
kissible	☐	kissable	☐
valuable	☐	valueible	☐
visable	☐	visible	☐

```
E  L  B  I  S  I  V  W  M  I  E  L  Q  H  W
S  G  V  Z  D  Q  Y  V  H  G  L  A  E  F  B
K  U  U  N  F  E  I  K  V  A  B  U  O  R  H
F  S  I  F  B  A  V  H  R  H  A  G  K  E  A
F  Q  S  T  H  B  S  M  J  U  U  H  J  L  I
X  N  N  D  A  K  Z  H  Y  I  L  A  K  B  A
N  X  D  U  I  B  I  G  I  F  A  B  R  I  A
Q  V  P  C  Y  N  L  S  X  O  V  L  H  S  G
D  V  J  S  E  T  W  E  S  U  N  E  J  S  F
E  L  B  I  R  R  E  T  P  A  O  A  N  O  Q
E  L  B  I  D  E  R  C  N  I  B  V  B  P  J
C  O  M  F  O  R  T  A  B  L  E  L  O  L  B
E  V  X  A  L  U  A  Z  X  V  G  T  E  Q  E
V  W  G  J  A  K  Q  J  W  J  J  Q  T  U  Y
J  K  Q  N  R  U  W  Y  M  K  C  B  U  P  N
```

Some Words Sound Alike, but...

The Difference Between "Stationary" and "Stationery"

Two words that sound and look very similar, but have very different meanings.

Stationary

This word means "standing still".

Examples using stationary:

The traffic was **stationary** on the motorway.

The human statue in the town square has been **stationary** now for six minutes.

Stationery

This word is associated with writing materials, paper and envelopes.

Examples using stationery:

The **stationery** cupboard contains paper, pens and envelopes.

Ask Trudie to make a list of the office **stationery**.

Tip: remember "e" for "e"nvelopes – envelopes are station"e"ry.

Is it "All" or "Al"?

Here are some words which mean different things, and are written in different ways, depending upon whether they have one 'l' or two.

All ready

All ready is used when you want to show you are prepared for something.

Examples using all ready:

He is packed and all ready to go the airport.

I am all ready for the argument that I know will happen.

Already

This is used when you want to talk about time which has past.

> **Examples using already:**
>
> I got to Jack's but he had already left.
>
> Monica has already passed her driving test.

All together

These words are used when you want to talk about a summary, or a whole.

> **Examples using all together:**
>
> All together there were 175 students present.
>
> All together, I have £1,700 worth of savings in two accounts.

Altogether

This is used when you mean completely or entirely.

> **Examples using altogether:**
>
> It is altogether (*entirely*) a different problem we now face.
>
> I find the whole subject altogether (*completely/entirely*) confusing.

All right

should be thought of as the opposite of "all wrong" and, as such, is two separate words.

> **Examples using all right:**
>
> **All right**, I am coming to help you.
>
> It is **all right** to ask Toni if you can share her text book.
>
> It will be **all right** once we settle into the new school.

A lot

"A lot" is the opposite of "a little", and as such, is two separate words.

Examples using a lot:

> Maria has **a lot** of books in her bedroom.

> There are **a lot** of people who live in poverty in the United Kingdom.

"Any one" or "Anyone"?

Any one

These words are used when you want to talk about an item in a group of things.

Examples using "any one":

> **Any one** of these paint colours would suit your kitchen.

> Take **any one** of these pens in order to complete the form.

Anyone

This means "any person at all".

Examples using "anyone":

> I do not want **anyone**, other than friends, at my party.

> If **anyone** can help me, I will be pleased.

Some Spelling Rules You Just Have to Learn

Sometimes there are spelling rules which you must learn.

Words which end in "e" lose the "e" when "ing" is added.

Examples:

Complete	Completing	Have	Having	Make	Making	Take	Taking
File	Filing	Love	Loving	Smile	Smiling	Tile	Tiling

The Plural Rule for Nouns Ending in "y"

See if you can spot the rules about words which end in "y" becoming "ies" when they become plural from the words in the list below. Clue: look at the letter immediately before the "y".

Alley	Alleys	Fly	Flies
Baby	Babies	Galley	Galleys
Boy	Boys	Hobby	Hobbies
Carry	Carries	Jetty	Jetties
Chimney	Chimneys	Monkey	Monkeys
Copy	Copies	Pony	Ponies
Family	Families		

THE RULE

When a word ends in "y" and has a *vowel* before it (a, e, i, o or u), then just add the letter "s".

When the word ends in a "y" and has a *consonant* (any letter other than a vowel) before it, then change the "y" to "ies".

Full or Ful?

What do you think is the rule relating to the following words?

Beautiful	Beautifully	Careful	Carefully
Faithful	Faithfully	Peaceful	Peacefully
Successful	Successfully	Regretful	Regretfully

THE RULE

When adding "ful" to a word USE ONLY ONE "L" – FUL.

When changing "ful" into "fully" USE TWO LETTER "L"s.

The Suffixes "ly" and "ment"

What do you think is the rule relating to the following words?

Accurate	Accurately	Desperate	Desperately
Separate	Separately	Achieve	Achievement
Replace	Replacement	Settle	Settlement
Sincere	Sincerely	Acknowledge	Acknowledgement

THE RULE

When adding "ly" or "ment" to words which end in "e" – keep the "e" in its place.

Exercise: I Can Find The Right Words

Decide which word of the following pairs is spelt correctly. Place a tick ✓ next to the correctly spelt word, **then find that word in the word search below.**

accidentaly	☐	accidentally	☐	immediatly	☐	immediately	☐
advertisment	☐	advertisement	☐	positively	☐	positivly	☐
arrangement	☐	arrangment	☐	removeing	☐	removing	☐
bodys	☐	bodies	☐	sincerely	☐	sincereley	☐
colourfull	☐	colourful	☐	storys	☐	stories	☐
extremely	☐	extremly	☐	trolleys	☐	trollies	☐
hopefuly	☐	hopefully	☐	vallies	☐	valleys	☐

Word Search

```
T A N G S U O S U R X A H T P Y P O
R N B L S E Y O Y Y C R N S O L Y R
X X E Z U E I L Y C D E J Y S L M D
S J P M L F E R I O M I L C I U Z D
V J B L E M R D O E K E A S T F A O
W B O B E S E U G T R L K E I E R K
Z R G R C N I N O E S V A I V P Q V
T Z T M T L A T C L Z Y K D E O M S
S X W A I R T N R B O J I O L H R V
E Y L I R W I T O E B C Z B Y R A G
T L X A E S F U H X V T J J R L P G
Y R E M O V I N G M B D Q B L W V Q
Y L E T A I D E M M I G A E S D Q B
H N B B R P P K G O X Z Y Y F Y G K
E C V P H E R I L W L S P I I Y Q V
G D M K Q B S S Q H P T U J E W G T
V I O X F Z O M A E K B K A A W L X
S X X Z G H I J P U C F U S H B D X
```

Speaking Skills

Most of the previous hints and tips have been related to, but not exclusively connected with, your writing skills.

When you speak it is equally important to be clear about your meaning so the audience understands your points.

The following pages contain tips that can help you speak confidently and correctly.

Of course each of these tips should be considered in your writing skills too!

Tautology

You may not have heard of tautology before, but it is something you will recognise when you understand its meaning:

> ### unnecessary repetition of meaning using different words.

Look at these examples and think how often you may have heard them, or used them.

1   The cake rose up in the tin.

2   The driver of the car reversed back.

Get the idea?

3   The bottle sank down into the sea.

I think you will know what it means now!

Example 1:   If something rises then it goes up — so "up" is unnecessary.

Simply say: The cake rose in the tin.

Example 2:   If something reverses it goes back — so "back" is unnecessary.

Simply say: The driver of the car reversed.

Example 3:   If something sinks it goes down — so "down" is unnecessary.

Simply say: The bottle sank into the sea.

Can you think of any more? Once you know this rule you will be aware that you hear examples of **tautology** more and more, and probably smile to yourself **and** avoid using them.

It is important when writing and speaking to make your words clear. Avoiding tautology is worth considering. It might, initially, make the reader or audience smile, but it will very soon annoy people. Here are some more common examples:

4   Will you repeat that again. *If you repeat an action you do it again, so "again" is unnecessary.*

48

5   I, myself, personally think that .... *I is sufficient, isn't it?*

6   I think the present is adequate enough. *Adequate means "sufficient or enough".*

7   We will have to co-operate together. *Co-operate means to do something together.*

8   Abrim linked together the clues and came up with the answer. *Linked means joined together.*

9   I shall still continue looking for that special gift for Emily. *Continue means to still do something.*

10   Please revert back to the previous statement. *Revert means to go back.*

Collective Nouns

It is a trend today for speakers to refer to groups of everything and anything as "bunches". I am sure you have all heard the phrase, possibly even used it, "a bunch of friends", or "a bunch of ideas".

Don't use the word "bunch" to describe a collection of anything except keys, grapes or flowers.

Here is a list of some long-standing and accepted collective nouns:

A herd of swans	A herd of deer	A swarm of bees
A flock of birds	A flock of sheep	A bunch of flowers
A bunch of keys	A bench of magistrates	A troupe of dancers
A company of actors	A band of musicians	A clump of trees

A fleet of cars.

Can you think of a collective noun for a group of students? Possibly an "assignment" of students, or a "chatter" of students!

How about a "stamp" of postmen?

Verb Tense Accuracy

What's wrong with this text?

The open air concert is being held next Friday and Saturday night in the park. The engineers, who are skilled at their job, is installing the loud speakers and public address systems that are being used by the bands and the organisers.

1   **being** is present tense. You say you are being cheeky, or he is being annoying. Yet the concert will take place in the future (next Friday and Saturday).

The correct tense to use is future tense. Hence you should write:

> The open air concert is **to be** held next Friday and Saturday night in the park.

2   **is** installing. Look at the sentence carefully. Who is doing the installing? The engineers.

If this is not easy to see, then read the sentence, missing out the phrase separated by the commas because the fact they are good at their job just gets in the way and is extra information you can do without.

Now it reads   *The engineers is installing* ....

Engineers is plural so the phrase should be:

> *The engineers* **are** *installing* ....

Put back the section separated by commas (that extra information you can do without) and the sentence reads

> *The engineers, who are skilled at their job, are installing* ....

3   **are being used** by the bands ....

As we discovered at the beginning of the paragraph, the concert is to be held in the future.

So the bands are **not** using the loudspeakers **now** as now is the present tense.

The sentence needs to reflect the future tense so you should write:

> public address systems that **will be used** by the bands and organisers.

Exercise

Try to correct the following sentences:

1   Whilst Melanie sits in the garden, the door bell rang.

2   The family hopes the plan to build a new home in the Algarve would work.

3   If the bicycle breaks, he would have to buy a new one.

4   By the time the cricket match started, everyone is thinking England will lose.

5   Hundreds of people will see the exhibition by the time it closed next week.

6   The Members of Parliament, whose average age is 48, is going to Brussels next week by EuroStar.

7   My garden has a number of hedgehogs, mainly in June and July, which is lovely to see.

8   Everyone thinks the plan, thought up by Bill and Trent, are likely to succeed.

9   The students, and their teacher, is trying Functional Skills for the first time this year.

10   Hamill wants to show his friends the photographs he takes on his holiday last year.

Almost the Last Word

Don't be tempted to pepper what you say with words such as "like", "basically", "actual/ly", obviously; "amazing", "awesome", etc.

You've all heard expressions such as:

"It was – **like** – raining this morning. I was – **like** – soaked through."

Clearly it was raining and the person was soaked and to suggest that it was like itself is silly. Don't use "like".

"I was – **like** – going up to town."

You are either going to town or not. Don't use "like".

"He was – **basically** – just helping me out."

What you mean is "He was helping me out." Don't use basically, it adds nothing to the sentence and annoys the listener.

"**Basically** – it's my fault."

"It's my fault" is sufficient.

"I was going to the – **actual** – station."

As opposed to the "virtual" station?

"I was actually pleased."

Why use "actually", saying you were pleased is clear enough.

"Obviously I'm going to the club tonight."

Unless when you say this to someone you are outside a club with your hand on the door, there is **nothing** obvious about the fact you are going to the club. Think about how you use "obvious".

For instance, if viewing a flooded village in Ethiopia where the villagers are living in tents it would be all right to say "Obviously these people are living in tents as their homes have been washed away in the flood." **That** really is **obvious.**

Amazing means **greatly surprising**. It is used correctly in a sentence such as "After the jumbo jet crashed into the Pacific Ocean the rescuers found it amazing that 150 people were alive in the sea."

So using amazing in a sentence like "Her dress was amazing" or "The concert was amazing", is incorrect.

Awesome means **causing wonder, breathtaking** or **inspiring dread**. It is used correctly in a sentence such as "The volcano erupted with awesome power."

So using awesome in a sentence like "It was an awesome song" is incorrect.

And Finally . . . .

Do think about what you say, the words you use and the message you want to convey.

Do **care** about what you say, the words you use and the message you want to convey.

For this Function Skills English Level 2 qualification you will need to show you can be clear and accurate in what you say and write. You must write and speak in a way that suits your audience. Writing an informal note to your mother about the things you'd like her to buy for you whilst she's out shopping is completely different to writing a formal job application letter. Speaking to your friends, using some slang words perhaps, is completely different from the need to address an audience when you go for a job interview and have to answer questions and look at people when doing so.

You have to learn to speak and write standard English and express your points of view effectively whether written or spoken. Take pride in your language — other people do.

Commonly Misspelt Words

This list of commonly misspelt words is included so you can refer to them quickly, but don't forget to also use your very good and indispensable friend **your dictionary**.

Word	word with different ending(s)	Word	word with different ending(s)
A		**B**	
A lot		Bachelor	
Absence	Absent	Balloon	Ballooning
Accommodate	Accommodation	Beauty	Beautiful
Achieve	Achievement	Begin	Beginner
Acknowledge	Acknowledgement	Believe	Believing
	Acknowledging	Benefit	Benefited
Acquire	Acquiring		Benefiting
Across		Burglar	Burglary
Address	Addresses	Business	
	Addressing		
Advertise	Advertising	**C**	
	Advertisement		
Agree	Agreement	Calendar	
	Agreeable	Careful	Carefully
All right		Carriage	
Already		Category	Categories
Altogether		Chief	Chiefly
Amount	Amounted	Circuit	
	Amounting	Colleague	
Analyse	Analysis	College	
	Analysing	Commemorate	Commemoration
Apparent	Apparently	Commission	Commissioner
Appear	Appearing	Compare	Comparison
	Appearance		Comparatively
Appropriate	Appropriately	Competent	Competently
Argue	Argument	Complete	Completely
	Arguing	Condemn	Condemning
Article			Condemnation
Associate	Association		Condemnatory
Attach	Attached	Conscience	
	Attachment	Consistent	Consistently
Attitude		Courteous	Courteously
Author		Curious	Curiously
Awkward	Awkwardly		Curiosity
	Awkwardness		

53

Word	word with different ending(s)	Word	word with different ending(s)

D

Daughter	
Decent	Decently
Decide	Decision
Defend	Defence
Definite	Definition
Democracy	
Descend	Descending
	Descendant
Despair	
Desperate	Desperately
	Desperation
Detached	
Deter	Deterrent
	Deterring
Deteriorate	Deterioration
Develop	Developing
	Development
Different	Differently
	Difference
Dilemma	
Disappear	Disappearance
	Disappearing
Disaster	Disastrous
Discipline	Disciplining
Disobey	Disobeying
	Disobedience
Duly	

E

Eight	Eighth
	Eighteen
Elegant	Elegantly
	Elegance
Embarrass	Embarrassing
	Embarrassingly
	Embarrassment
Endeavour	Endeavouring
Environment	Environmental
	Environmentally
	Environmentalist

Exaggerate	Exaggeration
Exceed	Exceedingly
Except	Exception
	Exceptionally
Excite	Excitement
	Exciting
Exercise	
Exhibition	
Existence	
Expense	Expensive
Experience	
Extraordinary	Extraordinarily
Extravagant	Extravagantly
	Extravagance
Extreme	Extremely

F

Fahrenheit	
Familiar	Familiarly
Favourite	
Feasible	
February	
Fiery	
Foreign	Foreigner
Fortune	Fortunate
	Fortunately
Forty	
Fourteen	
Friend	Friendly
	Friendliness
Fulfil	Fulfilment
	Fulfilling
Furniture	

G

Gallop	Galloping
	Galloped
Gauge	
Govern	Governing
	Government
	Governor

54

Word	word with different ending(s)	Word	word with different ending(s)
Grammar		Intelligent	Intelligence
Grievous			Intelligently
Guarantee	Guaranteeing	Intent	Intention
	Guarantor	Interest	Interesting
Guard	Guarding		Interested
		Irrelevant	
		Irresistible	

H

		J	
Harass	Harassing		
	Harassment	Jealous	Jealously
Heaven	Heavenly	Jewel	Jewels
Height			Jeweller
Heir	Heirloom		Jewellery
Hero	Heroes	Jeopardy	
Hinder	Hindrance		
Humour	Humouring		

K

Humour	Humouring
	Humorous
	Humorously
Hungry	Hungrily
Hygiene	Hygienic
	Hygienically

K	
Keen	
Keep	Keeper
	Keeping
Key	Keying
	Keyboard
Kiosk	
Know	Knowing
	Knowledge
	Knowledgeable

I

Identical	Identically
Illegible	Illegibly
Immediate	Immediately
	Immediacy
Imminent	Imminently
In between	
In fact	
In front	
Incident	Incidentally
Independent	Independently
	Independence
Infinite	Infinity
	Infinitely
Innocent	Innocently
	Innocence
Install	Installing
	Instalment
	Installation

L

Labour	Labouring
Laid	
Leisure	Leisurely
Liaise	Liaison
Liaising	
Lighten	Lightening
Like	Likely
	Liking
	Likelihood
Likewise	
Literature	

Word	word with different ending(s)	Word	word with different ending(s)
Loathe	Loathsome	Negotiate	Negotiating
Lonely	Loneliness		Negotiation
Lose	Losing	Neighbour	Neighbourly
Loose	Loosely		Neighbourhood
	Loosen	Ninth	
Lovely		No one	
Luxury	Luxurious	Notice	Noticing
			Noticeable
		Nuisance	

M

Maintain	Maintaining		
	Maintenance		

O

Manage	Managing	Occasion	Occasional
	Management		Occasionally
	Manageable		Occasioned
Marvel	Marvellous	Occur	Occurred
Mathematics	Mathematician		Occurring
Meant			Occurrence
Message	Messaging	Offer	Offered
	Messenger		Offering
Miniature		Old-fashioned	
Minute	Minutely	Omit	Omitting
Miscellaneous			Omission
Moderate	Moderation	Opportunity	Opportunities
	Moderately	Ordinary	Ordinarily
Moment	Momentarily	Original	Originally
	Momentary	Overrule	Overruling
Month	Monthly		
Most	Mostly		

P

Move	Moving		
	Movable	Paid	Payment
Multiple	Multiply	Paraffin	
		Parallel	Paralleled

N

		Paralyse	Paralysing
		Parliament	Parliamentary
Naïve	Naivety	Particular	Particularly
Necessary	Necessarily	Permanent	Permanently
Necessitate	Necessity	Permit	Permitting
Neglect	Neglectful		Permissible
	Negligent	Peruse	Perusal
	Negligence	Pigeon	

Word	word with different ending(s)	Word	word with different ending(s)
Poison	Poisoning	Reminisce	Reminiscence
	Poisonous	Repeat	Repeating
Prejudice	Prejudicial		Repetition
Prepare	Preparing	Resist	Resistible
	Preparation		Resistance
Present	Presence	Responsible	Responsibility
Pretence			Responsibly
Primitive		Restaurant	
Privilege		Rhyme	
Probable	Probably	Rhythm	
	Probability	Ridicule	Ridiculous
Procedure		Rogue	
Proceed	Proceeding	Rough	Roughly
Professor		Route	Routing
Pronounce	Pronouncing	Routine	Routinely
Proof	Prove		
Public	Publicly		
Punctuate	Punctuation		
Pursue	Pursuing		

Q

Quarter	Quarterly		
	Quartering		
Question	Questioning		
	Questionnaire		
Queue	Queuing		
Quiet	Quietly		
Quite			

S

Scene	Scenery
	Scenic
Scissors	
Secret	Secretly
Secretary	
Seize	Seizing
	Seizure
Sentence	
Separate	Separately
Silhouette	
Similar	Similarly
	Similarity
Sincere	Sincerely
	Sincerity
Skill	Skilful
Soldier	
Solicitor	
Souvenir	
Sovereign	Sovereignty
Speak	Speaking
Speech	
Statistics	Statistically
Subtle	Subtly
Success	Successful
	Successfully

R

Real	Really
	Reality
Receive	Receiving
Recommend	Recommending
	Recommendation
Refer	Referred
	Referring
	Referral
Referee	Reference
Refrigerator	
Religious	

Word	word with different ending(s)	Word	word with different ending(s)
Summary	Summarise Summarising	**V**	
Supersede	Superseding	Vary	Various Varying
Supervise	Supervising Supervisor Supervisory	Vacuum	
Surprise	Surprising	Value	Valuable
Survive	Survivor	Visible	Visibly Visibility
System	Systematic Systematically	Vegetable	
		Vengeance	
		Vicious	
T		Vigour	Vigorous Vigorously
Tariff		Villain	Villainous
Teach	Teacher Teaching	Virtual	Virtually
Technical	Technically Technician	**W**	
Technique		Wednesday	
Temperature		Weird	
Temporary	Temporarily	Whole	Wholly Wholesome
Tend	Tendency	Wield	Wielding
Terrify	Terrifying	Wilful	Wilfully Wilfulness
Tomorrow			
Tongue		Withhold	
Tragic	Tragically Tragedy	Wool	Woollen
True	Truly	**Y**	
Truth	Truthful Truthfully	Yacht	Yachting
Try	Tries	Yield	Yielding
Trying		Yesterday	
Twelfth			

U

Word	word with different ending(s)
Umbrella	
Undoubtable	Undoubtably Undoubted
Undue	
Unnecessary	Unnecessarily
Until	
Unusual	Unusually

58

SECTION 2

HOW DO I ....?

The skills you will need to learn and in which you will have to become competent in order to gain this Functional Skill qualification are described on page 1.

The skills are covered in the practice tasks in Section 3.

The Reference Sheets in this section provide opportunities for you to review and practise the skills for Functional English Level 2.

Completing Forms and Job Application Forms

In this section you will learn how to:

▶ read and summarise succinctly (R2.2)

▶ identify the purpose of texts (R2.3)

▶ read and actively respond to different texts (R2.5)

▶ present information concisely and clearly (W2.2)

When completing a form of any type, be it a form to open a bank account, or a mobile phone account, a student rail card, a passport, a holiday or a job application form, **accuracy** and **neatness** are vitally important.

Before you put pen to paper do the following:

✓ Study the form, all its questions and sections, so you know what information you will be expected to provide.

✓ If possible, photocopy the form, and practise filling it in. This will help you judge how large or small your writing should be in order to add the information required. It also shows you what your completed form will look like and help you decide if you can improve how you express your information and present your form.

✓ Carry out any research you need for the questions asked. For instance, you may have to provide information that you have stored somewhere; studying the form's questions alerts you to the fact that you need to **find that information**.

When completing the form do the following:

✓ Use **BLACK INK** and **BLOCK CAPITALS** – these guidelines are usually stated on the form and you will be aware of them having read it carefully and thoroughly before completing it.

✓ Use neat handwriting that is easy to read.

✓ Fill in every section – even if it means putting **Not Applicable** in some sections.

✓ Make sure you answer each question fully.

✓ Make sure you have deleted inapplicable information (usually indicated by an asterisk *) on the form, for instance *delete whichever is not applicable.

✓ Check your spelling is correct.

✓ Be honest.

✓ Keep a copy of the form before you send it off.

You will have to complete a variety of forms throughout your life. These simple guidelines will make that process easier and you will be confident of getting it right and portraying the right image.

Job Application Forms

The tips above apply equally to **job application forms**, but there are some extra points to consider.

Namely:

- Research the company carefully. You will probably be asked a question at interview that will check how much you know about the company, its product(s), partners, etc., and your research is vital.

- Read the job description carefully so you can be clear about what skills and qualities the employer sees as important. You can then make sure you include information on your application form to support the fact that you have some of these qualities and skills.

- Include details of qualifications you have achieved (don't include failures, your application form must concentrate on **positive** aspects).

- Confirm, before naming them, who your referees are to be. It is bad manners to quote someone's name as willing to give you a reference if you have not received their permission in the first place. They may refuse to act as referee if you do not clear it with them first.

- Be sure to include a **job reference number** if one was quoted in the advertisement.

- Use sentences rather than just bullet points throughout the form.

- Check, and double check, spelling, grammar and punctuation.

- Sound positive and enthusiastic.

- Do not lie.

- Take a copy of the form to refer to **before** the interview. You will probably apply for several jobs at the same time and you will need to remember what you said to each prospective employer.

- Return the form **well before the closing date**, and make sure you keep the form **clean, tidy and as uncrumpled** as possible.

The Purpose of Your Neatly, Accurately Completed Job Application Form

A prospective employer, on reading your form, should have a positive idea of the following:

- How your personality and qualities are suited to the job and the company.

- How your qualifications and skills are suited to the job and the company.

- How you have given your application careful consideration.

Completing an Accident Report Form

The completed accident report form on the following page gives details of an accident involving a member of staff at a plant nursery.

The intention is that relevant and accurate details will be recorded on the accident report form.

How do you set about deciding what to put on the form?

1   Read the text on the following page so you know what it is about.

2   Look at the accident report form to see what information needs to be included.

3   Be aware that on the accident report form you will only put facts. So read the text again and notice what is opinion or what is not relevant to the accident appears in **bold italics**. It is always important to be able to select fact from opinion.

4   Look at how the form has been completed. Would you have added anything else? Do you think all the facts have been included?

SUNFLOWER GARDEN CENTRE

<u>Accident Information</u>

❖ At 10:35 today Freya North was in the staff canteen, **which had just recently been re-opened after being relocated to the** first floor **from the ground floor.** Freya works in nursery number one.

❖ As Freya got to the till with her tray containing her **late** breakfast **of a plate of fried eggs, bacon and mushrooms** and a glass of fresh orange juice, the glass fell from the tray onto the floor. The glass broke and the orange juice spilt all over the floor.

❖ Freya stepped back **to avoid the orange juice spilling on to her skirt, which was new and the first time she had worn it**, and she slipped on the juice which had splashed to the floor and fell backwards, falling to the floor and twisting her left ankle.

❖ As she was still holding the tray when she slipped and fell, the plate of hot food landed in her lap.

❖ **Unable to stand up because of her injured ankle, Freya remained sitting on the floor with the hot food burning her legs through her skirt.**

❖ Jack Frost, from nursery number three, **had been sitting at a table near the till and had** witnessed the accident **as he finished his toast and pot of tea (because his break began 15 minutes before Freya's),** and he got up to help Freya off the floor **and support her whilst she stood on her right foot.**

❖ The canteen cashier, Maggie Pounder, who witnessed the accident, **used the telephone next to the till to** call Harris Woods the first aider from nursery number two. **The cashier would not have been able to do that in the old**

canteen as the phone was located near the entrance door and nowhere near the till, so it was lucky a telephone had been installed because she was able to ring immediately.

❖ At 10:45 Harris Woods arrived. **By this time Freya was sitting on a nearby chair, which someone had brought from the back of the canteen, near the window overlooking the fish pond, and Harris had helped her to get to.** Harris examined Freya's ankle.

❖ He decided Freya needed to see a doctor so asked the cashier to call an ambulance **so she could be taken to hospital.**

❖ **Freya was in pain and thought the ambulance seemed to take for ever to arrive but she was told afterwards that** it arrived at 11:00 **so it only took about 10 minutes after the call was made.**

❖ The paramedics from the ambulance took Freya to the Accident and Emergency department of the local hospital – Abbotsfield General – **and she sat for two hours in the Accident and Emergency Department before she was seen by a doctor. The doctor (Dr Benson) explained they had been very busy that morning and apologised for the delay.**

❖ Freya had an X-ray, **so she had to wait another 30 minutes. The X-ray** showed no broken bones, just a badly sprained ankle.

❖ Freya had minor burns to her upper legs **from the hot food that should have been her breakfast.**

❖ After advising rest for her ankle and giving her some ointment for her burns, the hospital sent Freya home at 13:05.

❖ **Her father left his work in a bank close to the hospital and picked her up to take her home in the family car.**

SUNFLOWER GARDEN CENTRE
ACCIDENT REPORT FORM

Date of Accident/Time of Accident	Where did the accident occur?
(Today's date, for instance)	Room *Staff Canteen*
11 September 2008 10:35am	Floor *First Floor*
Person(s) involved in the accident	Witness(es) of the accident/Department(s)
Freya North	Witness 1 Witness 2
Nursery No. 1	*Jack Frost* *Maggie Pounder, Canteen Cashier*
	Nursery No. 3

Accident Details and Outcome(s)

Whilst at the till paying for her breakfast, the glass of orange juice fell from the tray onto the floor. The juice spilt over the floor and Freya stepped back to avoid the juice hitting her skirt but she slipped in the juice on the floor. She fell to the floor and twisted her ankle. The hot food which had been on her tray fell into her lap and burnt her legs through her skirt.

Jack Frost witnessed the accident and helped Freya off the floor whilst Maggie Pounder, the cashier, called for Harris Woods, the first aider, to attend.

At 10:45am Harris Woods arrived and examined Freya's ankle. He asked Maggie Pounder to call an ambulance because he thought Freya needed to see a doctor.

The Ambulance arrived at 11:00am and took Freya to Abbotsfield General where she had an X-ray that showed she had a badly sprained ankle but no broken bones. She was advised to rest her ankle and given some ointment for the burns to her upper legs and sent home at 13:05.

Was a First Aider called?	Was treatment given by a First Aider?	If hospital treatment was given, please state:
Yes / No*	Yes / **No***	Admission to hospital?
Name and department of the person who called a first aider?		Yes / **No***
	Was an ambulance called?	Name of hospital
Harris Woods – Nursery No 2	**Yes** / No*	*Abbotsfield General*
Was a doctor called?		If Admission occurred, please state:
Yes / **No***		A&E/Ward*
		....
		Dr ....

Signature .... Date ....*(today's date)*..................

* delete whichever is not appropriate

Writing and Setting Out Memos

A memorandum (abbreviated to memo) – plural memoranda

> **In this section you will learn how to:**
> ▶ identify the purpose of texts (R2.3)
> ▶ detect point of view, implicit meaning and/or bias (R2.4)

A memo is an **internal** method of communication within an organisation.

Memos must be short documents, and usually deal with one subject. A long document within an organisation is usually sent in the form of a report.

The memo should be signed by the sender.

Memo 1

Although organisations have their own style of layout for memos, all memos contain these essential headings:

MEMORANDUM

To
From
Date
Subject
Copies to

Mrs A Winston, Personnel Manager

T Gilbert, Central Records Manager

15 June 2008

Lost file

Mr J Brown, Personnel Director
Miss P Patty, Central Records Clerk

Last week I informed you that Mrs Jane McTavish's file had been lost or mislaid.

I am pleased to report that this has now been found and I have written to Mrs McTavish apologising for the delay in confirming the details she requested.

I am sorry for the inconvenience this has caused all parties.

Trevor Gilbert

Trevor Gilbert

The subject of the memo has been identified.

This section indicates who else, other than the named recipient, has received a copy.

Typical layout of a memorandum (memo). This is formal as it includes their titles (Mr, Mrs, Personnel Manager, etc.).

The **purpose** of this document is to **give information**. What are the clues?

1   The **first paragraph** has the words "I informed you that......" these are key words that indicate some further information is about to be given.

2   The **second paragraph** gives updated information and the key words to notice are "I am pleased to report ...." at the beginning of the sentence. This indicates to the reader a successful outcome and that some information is about to be given.

3   Another phrase in the **second paragraph** indicating details of action taken is "I have written ......".

All these phrases indicate a document that gives information to the reader.

In this example you can see the message is short and simple and deals with only one point.

Who the memo is from, and to whom it is being sent, are identified and the document is dated and signed.

Memo 2 - another formal memo

MEMORANDUM

To   Jamil Sunni, Car Park Manager

From   Catherine Woodleigh, Personnel Assistant

Date   28 September 2008

Re   Car Parking Arrangements

The new car parking arrangements came into operation on 20 September and I outlined the new procedures in my memo dated 15 August. This memo clearly described the system and the duties you would be required to undertake.

Unfortunately, it has come to my attention that despite my requests, you have not been following my instructions. I have had a number of complaints from staff who have been unable to park in their allotted space because they have found it already occupied. Additionally, some staff have been unable to use the car park as the barrier does not operate with their key card.

This state of affairs is unacceptable and I wish you to attend a meeting with me on Wednesday 30 September at 9.15am with a view to discussing these, and other, problems that have occurred since the introduction of the new system.

Catherine Woodleigh

Catherine Woodleigh

The **purpose** of this document is to **make a complaint**. What are the clues?

1. The **first paragraph** describes the background/topic of the memo.

2. The **second paragraph** uses the key words "unfortunately", "it has come to my attention" and "despite". All these words are rarely used in a document that aims to convey that everything is all right.

3. The **third paragraph** uses the key words "state of affairs is unacceptable " and goes on to give an instruction to attend a meeting at a set day and time, without offering the opportunity of checking this is convenient or rearranging. All these are clues that something is definitely not right.

Clearly, the writer of this document is dissatisfied.

Informal Memo

This is an example of an **informal** memo:

MEMORANDUM

To	Janet Markham, Advertising Department
From	Catherine Woodleigh, Purchasing Department
Date	15 June 2008
Re	Company's Sales Brochure

The 2,000 copies of the company's Christmas brochure have been received from the printer today.

These are available for you to collect at your earliest convenience.

Catherine

In this example, the names have no title and there are no job titles included – although people's departments are shown. This is important because an organisation could employ people with the same name but who work in different departments.

The memo is dated. There is a subject – this time expressed as 're' (short for 'reference').

The memo is signed with the sender's first name only – the surname could be included.

Taking Messages

It is always helpful to use a standard message form to record a message, whether it is a telephone message or a message of another kind. The headings on a standard form will help you include the information needed.

There is a message form on the following page, but this is not the only layout that companies use.

Remember you should always:

- Use simple, straightforward words.

- Keep your sentences short but vary the length a little so that the message reads well.

- Include **all, and only, the key facts and information.**

- Leave out irrelevant information.

- If you are repeating a request for the reader of the message to **do something,** make it a request, **not an order.**

- Be very specific and clear about days, dates and times. If you have to give a non-specific time, e.g. "tomorrow", add the day and date in case your message is not read immediately. It is advisable to always be specific about days and dates in order to avoid confusion.

- Mark urgent messages clearly.

Your responsibility does not end when you place the message on the right desk – it only ends when the person has read it and understood it.

Identifying the Key Facts

Every message contains key facts. If you miss them out of the message it will not make sense – or not make **complete sense.**

Business callers are normally quite good at giving the key facts in an ordered way and checking them through afterwards. Private callers may be less helpful and some may like to chat, so that it becomes difficult to sort out what is important from what is not.

A good way to check you have the message clear in your mind is to read back your summary to the caller. This both checks that you have the message correctly with all the important facts, and gives the caller the opportunity to alter or add anything.

MESSAGE FORM

TO..DEPARTMENT ....

DATE ....TIME ....

CALLER'S NAME ....

ORGANISATION ....

TELEPHONE NUMBER ....FAX NUMBER ....

EMAIL ADDRESS...

✓ Appropriate box(es)

      Telephoned   ☐

      Returned your call   ☐

      Called to see you   ☐

      Left a message   ☐

      Requests you call back   ☐

      Please arrange an appointment   ☐

Message

....

....

....

....

....

....

Taken by.................................... Department.................................... Time..................

Using Images in Communication

In this section you will learn how to:

▶ present information on complex subjects concisely and clearly (W2.2)

▶ use a range of different styles of writing for different purposes (W2.3)

Images can be used to enhance and explain written communications.

Remember, use images **to enhance the text** and to help the reader's understanding of the text. An image may also provide information in addition to text. **An image should not be included if it has no relevance.**

Think carefully about why you are using images and only use appropriate images in appropriate places.

Presenting Numerical Data in Visual Form

It is important to recognise that presenting information in just one way might not suit every reader.

In the first two examples, which present information on temperatures in Europe, some people will find it easier to understand the information in the table, whilst others prefer to see a graph or a chart.

Therefore, the **purpose** of including the chart **and** the table in the document is to allow the reader to interpret the information in the way they can best understand.

Example 1

Data in tabular (table) form

EUROPEAN TEMPERATURES 14 FEBRUARY	
Prague	13
Helsinki	8
Oslo	6
Stockholm	10
Madrid	16
Lisbon	14
Warsaw	7

Example 2

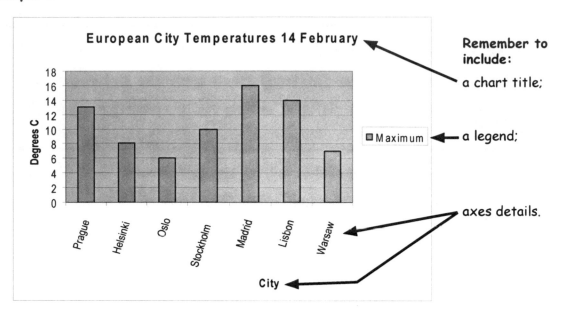

European City Temperatures 14 February

Remember to include:

a chart title;

a legend;

axes details.

Using Images in Text

Advertisement 1

Including an image to attract readers and encourage bookings:

CRUISING ON THE AIDAdiva

Imagine ...... it's 9.30 in the morning and your luxury cruise liner has just docked in yet another picturesque Mediterranean harbour. You have just finished breakfast in one of the three restaurants on the top deck of the vessel and looking out of your cabin window you can see yet another picturesque island waiting to be explored.

The forecast for the day ahead is 27° and you have until your cruise liner leaves port at 9pm to explore today's destination.

Don't leave it to your imagination:

Come and experience the relaxing life on board this newest addition to the AIDA* fleet

Telephone: Sailaway Cruises on 01855 6775520
for full cruising information

* AIDAdiva's sisters include:
AIDAbella. AIDAaura, AIDAcara, AIDAvita, AIDAluna

Advertisement 2

In this instance, the *text* is being used to give additional information about four areas of the country:

WEATHER UK
20th February 2008

WEATHER UK
20th February 2008

Norfolk and Suffolk

There are few clouds at 2000 feet

Visibility is 7000m

Cornwall and Devon

Light rain at 1300 feet

Broken rain clouds at 1600 feet

Wind speed 18-36 mph

Writing Advertisements

Advertisements may be placed in newspapers or magazines for a number of reasons, including:

- to advertise jobs;
- to promote products or services;
- to announce special events or functions;
- to publicise changes in an organisation;
- to recall faulty goods.

The **classified advertisements** section of a newspaper allows quick reference to a wide range of advertisements, which are usually inserted according to subject.

Line Advertisements

> GOOD BUY, BRAND new telephone/fax/
> copier/scanner for sale.   Owner is relocating
> abroad. Tel: 0184 576399

This information runs from line-to-line, often using the same typeface throughout, with no special layout. Charges are made by the line, normally with a minimum charge for three or four lines.

In such advertisements (also know as lineage ads), an opening should be made that catches the readers' attention, and then as much abbreviated information as possible should be contained in as few lines as possible.

Display Advertisements

These may use a variety of fonts and sizes, and may be illustrated with artwork and colour. Charges are based on the number of column centimetres, often with a minimum size. Information can be displayed within the advertisement to attract attention to special features.

Porto Santo Lines

£35

ONE DAY CRUISE

Discover a new island. Porto Santo Line offers you an unforgettable one-day package, aboard the ship "Lobo Marinho".

Travel with us and find out why Porto Santo is called the "Golden Island". Contact us today to make your reservation.

**Porto Santo Lines, Rua da Praia 6, Funchal, Madeira
Tel/Fax 291 228 662**

Column Advertisements (in newspapers and magazines)

The pages of newspapers and magazines are divided into **columns** and advertisers purchase so many column widths. The publisher charges so much per column and depth of advertisement.

In the following example the page has been divided into four columns. Hop, Skip and Jump has taken an advertisement over two columns.

	HOP, SKIP AND JUMP
	Shoe manufacturers of quality
	END OF SEASON SALE
	Leather Uppers • Leather Soles
	• Luxury Comfort Linings

Sizes 5, 6, 7, 8, 9, 10 and 11.

Brogue Black	Brogue Brown
Oxford Black	Oxford Brown
Casual Black	Casual Brown
Lace Black	Lace Brown

Telephone to place an order TODAY
Whilst stocks last

0165 7873 9882

Designing Advertisements

Designing an advertisement is an exercise in **summarising**. It is important to pick out the main points, features, advantages, or whatever is relevant to the theme of the advertisement.

It is essential to ensure the advertisement will be **seen** on the page of the newspaper or magazine. If it is displayed unattractively, it will not achieve this objective. Here are some guidelines:

- ✓ Use a company logo, prominently displayed. People can identify with a well-known logo.

- ✓ Whatever is being advertised, display the headline **PROMINENTLY** using bold text, underlining, or **ALL CAPITALS**, for instance.

- ✓ Break up the information sensibly and logically; perhaps various points could be listed using an asterisk or a bullet point.

- ✓ Use spacing and balance sensibly — remember the more space you use the more you will pay!

- ✓ Try to achieve a progressive display which categorises information logically, leading finally to action required by the reader — "visit us on ???" "contact us", etc.

Writing and Setting Out Business Letters

In this section you will learn how to:

▶ identify the purpose and meaning of texts (R2.3, R2.4)

▶ present information and ideas concisely, logically and persuasively (W2.1)

▶ write a range of documents suited to the purpose and audience (W2.3)

▶ use a range of sentence structures, including complex sentences (W2.4)

A business letter is an **external** method of communication and reflects how an organisation communicates with, and is viewed by, people and organisations outside the business.

There are a number of purposes for business letters:

✓ providing information;

✓ giving instructions;

✓ confirming arrangements;

✓ improving customer services;

✓ public relations.

A business letter has three parts:

1   introductory paragraph;

2   middle paragraph(s);

3   closing paragraph.

Introductory Paragraph

The introduction/opening paragraph introduces the theme/purpose of the letter and puts it into a context or provides a background.

Introductory paragraphs are also used to mention essential people, events or things to which the letter will refer.

Middle Paragraph(s)

These provide detailed information.

The middle paragraphs of a letter **develop a theme** and **provide all relevant details** and particulars. The number of paragraphs used will depend upon the complexity of the letter's subject. However, paragraphs should be kept fairly short and deal with only one topic at a time. **New topic = new paragraph** is something you must keep in mind.

Closing Paragraph

This provides an action statement and a courteous close.

In this paragraph you will attempt to summarise your comments and state what action you will take, or wish to be taken.

Some letters are concluded with a courteous sentence to act as a means of signalling the end of the document.

WITH CARE
AIR CARGO HANDLING PLC

Hangar 18R, Manchester Airport, Manchester MR4 6JE
0161 346 98667
email: withcare@manair.aviation.com

Ⓐ

Ⓑ

23 March 2008

Mr Peter Phillips
Despatch Department Manager
Mercury Components plc
Unit 7
Coniston Industrial Park
BARNSLEY
South Yorkshire
SO13 6BN

Ⓒ

Dear Mr Phillips

Ⓓ

Ⓔ

Ⓕ

AIR FREIGHT TO CHICAGO 4 April 2008

Thank you for your company's recent request to quote for transporting a packing crate to Chicago.

As you know, our Mike Richards came to your organisation yesterday to examine the crate, take its measurements and establish its weight. As a result of his visit we are pleased to be able to quote the sum of £568.90 + VAT. Our formal quotation is enclosed with this letter.

For this sum we will:

Ⓖ

- collect the crate on 2 April before 12 noon

- transport it to our depot at Manchester Airport

- ensure the paperwork for its journey is in order

- obtain UK Customs clearance for the crate

- put it on flight WC457 departing at 15:20 hours on 4 April, for Chicago O'Hare Airport

- upon arrival, arrange for our American handlers to unload the crate and obtain US Customs clearance

- store safely in the depot until your US client collects the crate.

We trust this quotation is acceptable and look forward to assisting you on this occasion. We would need confirmation of your wish to employ our services no later than 28 March.

Ⓗ

If you wish to discuss this matter further, please do not hesitate to contact me.

My direct line number is 0161 346 2323.

Yours sincerely

Ⓘ

Paul Falcon
Procurement Manager
Enc

Ⓙ

Key to Parts of a Business Letter

(A) The **letter heading** of the company including a company logo.

(B) **Date** expressed as dd/mm/yyyy.

(C) **Name, title** and **company name** and **address** of the person and company receiving the letter.

(D) **Salutation** – Dear Mr Phillips because the letter is addressed to him in the name and address line.

(E) **Heading**: indicating what the letter is about.

(F) **Introductory paragraph.**

(G) **Middle paragraphs** providing details.

(H) **Closing paragraphs** providing an action statement and a courteous close.

(I) **Complimentary close**: Yours sincerely because the recipient's name is used in the salutation. The writer's name and title, leaving space for his signature!

(J) **Enc** indicating there is an enclosure.

Useful Phrases for Business Letters

Thank you for your letter dated ....

As you may know, ...

I wish to inform you that ....

I was pleased to hear that ....

I wish to enquire about ....

I should like to place an order for ....

I look forward to hearing from you in the near future.

I should be grateful if you would kindly send me ....

Following our recent telephone conversation, I wish to ....

Please do not hesitate to let me know if I can do anything further to help ....

Business Letter 1

SETHCOTE STATIONERY AND COMPUTING SUPPLIES

Sethcote House: Bamfield Way: YOUR TOWN YW3 5BK

01662 4522128   www.sethcote.stationery.co.uk

17 October 2008

Mr I Curlish
7 Pine Ridge Road
YOUR TOWN
YW14 5BP

Dear Mr Curlish

Thank you for your recent enquiry concerning the photo quality paper we stock at Sethcote Stationery and Computing Supplies.

We are pleased to give you the details you have requested.

We have the following products available:

Gloss A4 size	packet of 20 sheets	£6.49
Matt A4 size	packet of 100 sheets	£7.99
Satin A4 size	packet of 20 sheets	£6.50
Gloss 6 x 4 size	packet of 20 sheets	£1.99
Matt 6 x 4 size	packet of 50 sheets	£2.50

For those customers who find it inconvenient to come into the store, we offer a next-day postal delivery service for all our paper products at the quoted cost, **plus** £2.50 postage and packing.

If we can be of any further assistance please do not hesitate to let us know. We look forward to being of service to you.

Yours sincerely

Seth Cotefield

Seth Cotefield

The **purpose** of this document is to **give information**. It also states facts. What are the clues?

1   The **first paragraph** has the words "Thank you for your recent enquiry". This gives a clue that the person receiving this letter has been asked for information and that **this** document being written will contain information.

2   The **second paragraph** uses the key words "We are pleased to give you details". Once again, this indicates the letter will give information.

3   The **purpose** of the document is to **give information** to **someone who understands the subject** – in this case paper quality and sizes. The writer has presented the information on the paper prices in a style that is easy to follow and that stands out from the other text of the letter. The recipient is able to see, at a glance, the main information that was requested.

In this way the document meets the **purpose** and the **audience**.

4   **Paragraph four** gives <u>additional information</u> that the customer may not have known and may find useful. This information is used to **persuade** the customer to buy.

5   **Paragraph five** is a polite way of ending a letter that gives information and is also a way of creating an impression of being helpful, together with encouraging custom. The key words are "If we can be of any further assistance", "please do not hesitate to let us know", and "we look forward to being of service to you".

> NOTE: The letter uses "we" throughout. It is important not to begin with "we" (the company or organisation) then change to "I" (the writer) half way through. You must be consistent.

Business Letter 2

BROOKFIELD
BOROUGH
COUNCIL

11 November 2008

The Proprietor
Painted Ladies Hair Stylist
66 High Road
YOUR TOWN
YV5 4GG

Dear Madam

It has come to the attention of this Council that you have placed a notice in the first floor windows of the property you occupy at 66 High Road, Your Town. This notice covers all three windows facing the High Road and acts as an advertisement for your business.

Unfortunately this notice contravenes the local bylaw 55c (sub-sections 9 – 12), which clearly states that business names and details must only be displayed on the **ground floor** and above the shop doorway(s). Accordingly this letter gives you notice to remove the offending addition to your property **no later than 10 am on 15 November**. Failure to comply with this request will result in your business being fined the sum of £2,200 per day for each day the notice remains after 14 November.

A copy of the relevant bylaw is enclosed for your information.

Yours faithfully

J Allan

J Allan
Assistant Solicitor

Enc

The **purpose** of this document is to **give information and request a necessary course of action**. It also states facts. What are the clues?

1 **Paragraph 1** begins with the phrase "It has come to the attention ....". This phrase rarely means the reader will hear anything good. In this case the reader is about to receive a warning. The phrasing of the letter is very formal – which means polite but to the point and allowing no room for negotiation.

2 **Paragraph 2** contains a further clue with the word "unfortunately", which rarely means good news.

3 The information is presented clearly and logically because the first paragraph states the nature of the problem and the second paragraph details why it is a problem, giving information about what must be done, by when and what will occur if this action is not taken.

NOTE: It is important in your writing that the subject and the verb agree.

An example of this is the wording in Paragraph 2 – "Unfortunately this notice contravenes the local bylaw 55c (sub-sections 9 – 12), which clearly **states** that ...." You might think "states" should be "state" because "state" agrees with "sub-sections". However, this would be incorrect.

Here is it important to look at what the word "states" relates to. The sentence could be written as "Unfortunately this notice contravenes the local bylaw 55c, which states that ....". It is the bylaw 55c that states something.

Using the Telephone and Making Telephone Calls

Before You Place a Call

✓   Think about what you wish to say and how you will say it. Courtesy is expected when using the telephone just as if you are talking in person.

✓   Make a list of what you need to say and the information you need to give and/or receive **before placing the call. BE PREPARED.**

✓   Dialling too quickly may be the cause of dialling a wrong number. Never just hang up. Apologise and let the person who answered the telephone know you have dialled the incorrect number.

How to Speak on the Telephone

✓   When speaking, think of the way you sound. On the telephone sounds and moods are magnified. **Talk with a smile in your voice.** The person on the other end of the telephone cannot see your facial expressions and your tone of voice will need to express politeness, enthusiasm and efficiency.

✓   Make sure you say your words clearly and precisely. It is embarrassing, and time-wasting, to be asked to repeat what you are saying. Names and addresses are particularly difficult, so say yours slowly, spelling any unusual words.

Making Telephone Calls

✓ It is polite, and necessary, to identify yourself. If you are calling from a company, then you would need to identify your company, your name, and perhaps your department, before going on to say why you are calling. For instance:

Good morning, this is Blackwood and Company of York. Janet speaking from the Purchasing Department. I am ringing to place an order...... I wish to speak to ....

How to Answer a Ringing Telephone

✓ The proper way to answer the telephone is give a greeting – **hello; good afternoon** – followed by identifying your telephone number if it is your home, or your name and your company. **Never** answer with just "hello" or "yes". Hello is useless because it does not tell the caller anything, and "yes" is curt and impolite, and again it does not tell the caller anything – except perhaps that you are in a bad mood and cannot be bothered.

Good Manners on the Telephone

✓ Answer a ringing telephone promptly.

✓ If you dial a number that is wrong, apologise promptly and hang up.

✓ Calling a business at or very near closing time is thoughtless and not likely to result in a successful call.

✓ Introduce yourself when placing a call.

✓ Answer a phone by identifying yourself, your company and/or your department.

✓ When speaking to anyone who is working and for whom time is important, make your call informative and short – plan ahead.

✓ It is polite to let the person who **made** the call **end** the call.

Sending Faxes

Facsimile Transmission

A fax is an efficient and speedy method of communication and can be used to send text and images. However, there are some important points to consider when sending a fax.

When and What to Fax

Always make sure the message is clear and take into account the following:

- Only send faxes when communication is **URGENT**. Email would be another suitable method of urgently communicating something, but a fax can be used when someone does not have email.

- **Don't count on privacy** – remember that it is not always the case that the person to whom the fax is being sent has their own fax machine. Most companies have centrally placed fax machines. For this reason be aware that the message can be seen and read by anyone. Do not send sensitive or confidential information in this way.

Always use a **Fax Cover Sheet**. It should contain the following information:

- The receiver's name and fax number.

- Your name, your business name, address, telephone number and fax number.

- The date (and possibly time).

- The total number of pages being transmitted, including the cover sheet. When you list the number of pages, it means the recipient can check that all pages have been received.

- A list of what you are faxing to ensure that the other party receives everything you've faxed.

- Cover sheets may also include special notations, such as "Urgent" and "For Immediate Delivery".

Some things do not fax well:

- Limit the use of dark colours as they increase transmission time and use the recipient's ink!

- Do not use light colours for text as they may not be seen by the fax machine as dark enough to register.

- Try to avoid colour images and photographs in faxes.

Fax Cover Sheet

Clearly mark who the fax is **to**. (If the company to which you are sending the fax has a centrally placed fax machine, make sure the fax gets to the right person by clearly identifying the recipient's name and job title.)

Include the **fax number**. (If your company has a central fax machine, it may not be you who sends the fax, but a telephonist. Make sure she/he can see the fax number clearly.)

Give your name.

Include your fax number.

Remember to count the front cover as page 1.

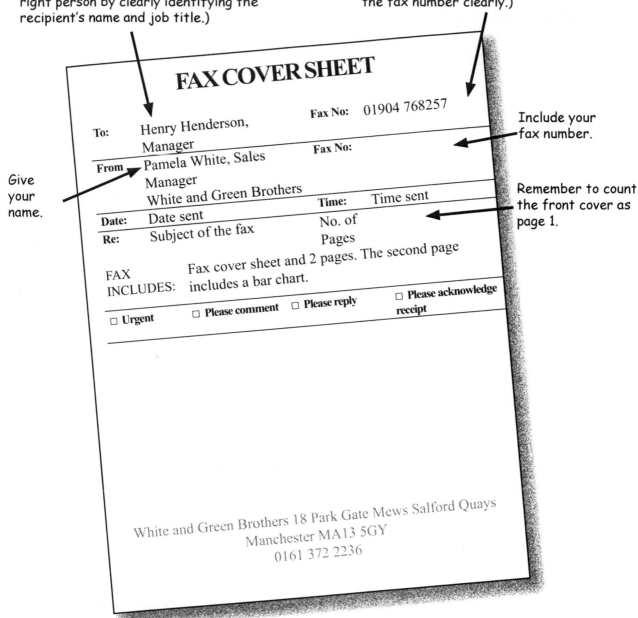

FAX COVER SHEET

Fax No: 01904 768257

To: Henry Henderson, Manager

Fax No:

From Pamela White, Sales Manager

White and Green Brothers

Time: Time sent

Date: Date sent

No. of Pages

Re: Subject of the fax

FAX INCLUDES: Fax cover sheet and 2 pages. The second page includes a bar chart.

☐ Urgent   ☐ **Please comment**   ☐ **Please reply**   ☐ **Please acknowledge receipt**

White and Green Brothers 18 Park Gate Mews Salford Quays
Manchester MA13 5GY
0161 372 2236

Writing and Setting Out Personal Letters

A personal letter is a letter written from someone's home address to either:

✓ a company – for instance to accompany a job application, or to complain about something; or

✓ a friend – for instance to invite a friend to stay with you.

Some Points to Remember About Letter Writing

✓ **Firstly: the date.**

Put the date the letter is written. This date should be shown as: dd/mm/yyyy

that is: 14th June 2008. Do not mix this order.

✓ **Secondly: the name and address to where the letter is being sent.**

Remember to write to a person if you can;

that is: Mr Jaz Allahan.

If you don't know the name of the person, address the letter to a job title;

that is: The Marketing Manager.

> *If it is an informal letter to a friend, it is acceptable to omit the name and address.*

> **Remember:** Don't just write Allahan and Corby Ltd. A COMPANY cannot open a letter, but a PERSON can!

✓ **Thirdly: who are you writing to?**

When you write "Dear ...." it is called the salutation.

When you write "Yours ...." it is called the complimentary close.

The salutation and complimentary close must match;

that is: Dear Mr Jones = Yours sincerely

            Dear Sirs = Yours faithfully

When you use a person's name, be sincere!

> *In an informal letter to a friend you can write "Dear Patrick".*

> **Note:** Only the word *Yours* has a capital letter at the beginning.

✓ **Fourthly: sign the letter.**

A letter from you needs to be signed. After the complimentary close, leave yourself space for a signature, then print your name. This is important because your signature may not be readable and the person who receives the letter will not know your name.

> *If it is an informal letter to a friend you just need to write "Best wishes" or "Kind regards" and sign your first name.*

Examples of Address, Salutation and Complimentary Close

Name and address:	Mr P Marks Sunningbrow Golf Course Sunningbrow Hill Aberdeen AB7 3NH
Salutation:	Dear Mr Marks
	Never write Dear Mr P Marks – just Dear Mr Marks. Think of how you would address him if meeting him. You would say "Mr Marks", so write it as you would say it.
Complimentary close:	Yours sincerely
	You have used his name, so be SINCERE!

Name and address:	The Sales Manager McKie and Aston plc 8 School Fields York YO14 5ND
Salutation:	Dear Sir or Madam
	because you have not used a name
Complimentary close:	Yours faithfully
	You have not used a name, so how can you be SINCERE!

Name and address:	Mrs K Trent Office Manager T&N Agency Villamoura Road Bexhill on Sea Sussex SX5 7BQ	This time you have used a name and a job title.
Salutation:	Dear Mrs Trent	
	because you have addressed the letter to her	
Complimentary close:	Yours sincerely	
	You have used her name, so be SINCERE!	

A Personal Letter Written to a Company

> ## In this section you will learn how to:
>
> ⊳ use a range of different styles of writing for different purposes (W2.3)
>
> ⊳ present information/ideas, concisely, logically and persuasively (W2.1)
>
> ⊳ use a range of sentence structures, including complex sentences (W2.4)

Letter 1

The following is an example of a personal letter written to a company:

Writer's home address or return address. Don't put your name here.

The address and telephone number/email address can be:

- in the centre;
- at the right hand side;
- at the left hand side; or
- a combination as seen in this example.

6 Telford Drive
Hightown
Wiltshire
HT4 7VV

Telephone: 01652 974356
Email: trevor@communication.co.uk

12 April 2008

Always begin with the date (dd/mm/yyyy).

The Secretary
Hightown Drama Society
The Strand Theatre
Hightown
Wiltshire
HT2 3GG

Dear Sir or Madam

I wish to enquire if your society has any vacancies for someone who is a keen amateur dramatist?

In June I will be completing a two-year drama course at Hightown Community College and, before I start university in October, I would be keen to gain experience in a theatre. This last year at college I have particularly enjoyed working behind the scenes and would appreciate any experience of this type, if available.

I look forward to perhaps hearing from you in due course and thank you for considering my request.

Yours faithfully

Leave yourself space for a signature.

Trevor Moore

What do you think was the main purpose of Letter 1?

Was it to give information? Was it to ask for information? Was it to apply for a job?

It was mainly to make an enquiry about vacancies which might be suitable for Trevor Moore. The clue for the reader is in the **first paragraph** with the phrase used at the very beginning, "I write to enquire". Immediately the recipient (the reader) knows they will have to respond to the letter because it asks a question.

The writer has stated **in the first paragraph** the purpose of the letter and the nature of the enquiry. This presents the information **clearly and logically.**

In the second paragraph the writer goes on to **persuade** the reader why this enquiry should be looked upon favourably because he gives information about his experience and interests that are relevant to his enquiry. This aims to persuade the reader he is suitable and that Hightown Drama Society cannot do without Mr Trevor Moore!

The words in the **final paragraph** that indicate a response is expected are "I look forward to perhaps hearing from you ....". It would be impolite for the drama society not to acknowledge the letter.

So, if you want a reply to a letter you write, consider using the same words as Trevor.

An Informal Personal Letter to a Friend

> ## In this section you will learn how to:
>
> ▶ use a range of different styles of writing for different purposes (W2.3)
>
> ▶ present information/ideas, concisely, logically and persuasively (W2.1)
>
> ▶ ensure written work has accurate grammar, punctuation and spelling and the meaning is clear (W2.6)
>
> ▶ use a range of sentence structures, including complex sentences (W2.4)

Letter 2

The following is an example of an informal personal letter written to a friend:

Writer's home address, or return address. Don't put your name here. →

Middlebank Farm
Trum Gelli
Gynedd
GY11 15MK
Wales

07751345 678
pigriffiths22@farmstead.co.uk

The address and telephone number/email address can be:

- in the centre;
- at the right hand side;
- at the left hand side.

9 June 2008

Dear Molly

I received your letter just today, even though you posted it first class on 2nd June!

It was great to hear all your news. I imagine you are quite excited about being chief bridesmaid for Julia. Fortunately your sister has consulted you about the colour and style of dress and, I must say from your description, it sounds lovely – not too embarrassingly fussy!

Mother and father say to send their best wishes to Julia for 2nd July, and of course they wish her and Graeme a happy married life.

Once the wedding is over you must come and stay for a few days before we fly to Mauritius in August. Just let me know and we'll arrange to meet you at the station.

I've lots to tell you but it can wait until I see you in August. I don't suppose you have thought of what you are going to take to Mauritius, whereas I have metaphorically packed and unpacked my case dozens of times!

See you soon.

Best wishes

Pam

Leave yourself space for a signature.

This letter is a personal letter to a friend. It is 'chatty' but still uses good grammar, spelling and punctuation. **Do not be tempted to use abbreviations like you use in text messaging.**

The language is less formal than the other letters you have so far read in this book, but what Pam wishes to convey to Molly is structured logically.

The **first paragraph** takes the form of a general, informal greeting between friends.

The **second paragraph** talks about a forthcoming wedding that Molly is attending as bridesmaid.

The **third paragraph** sends good wishes to Molly's sister from Pam's parents.

The **fourth and fifth paragraphs** move logically to plans for after the wedding.

The **final paragraph** is a brief, friendly "See you soon" greeting.

It's acceptable to be informal between friends but you would not phrase a formal letter in this way.

Writing Reports

In common with any other business document, a report needs to be planned and, before beginning, you must consider the following:

- A report will usually be requested by people who need the information for a specific purpose.

- A report differs from an essay in that it is designed to provide information that will be acted on, rather than to be read by people interested in the ideas for their own sake. Because of this, it has a different structure and layout.

- **Do not write in the first person.**

- **Use the past tense to describe your findings.**

    "It was found that......... etc., etc". **It** rather than **I** and the past tense of the verb to find, i.e. **found.**

Points to Consider Before Beginning your Report

For whom am I writing the report?

- A named individual, or a group of people?

- Person(s) who have no knowledge of the subject matter?

- What do the readers need to know?

- What do the readers already know?

What is my objective?

- ✓ To inform the readers?

- ✓ To explain ideas?

- ✓ To persuade?

- ✓ To consult?

- ✓ To transmit ideas or information, facts or findings?

- ✓ To make recommendations about ways of doing things, making improvements or changes?

What is the context?

- ✓ Urgent/important?

- ✓ Routine or "one-off"?

- ✓ Stand alone, or linked with a presentation?

- ✓ Sensitive?

What source material?

- ✓ Is it readily available?

- ✓ Do I need to do any research?

If you skip the planning stage, poor preparation invariably causes time-consuming problems at a later stage.

Structuring a Report

A report is used for reference and is often quite a lengthy document. It has to be clearly structured for you and your readers to quickly find the information it contains.

Parts of a Report

The nature of the report will vary from routine reports to complex, non-routine reports. The layout will vary too, yet all reports should have the following common features:

Cover Sheet

This should contain the following:

- ✓ full title of the report;

- ✓ your name;

- the name of the person(s) for whom the report is intended;
- the date.

Terms of Reference

This refers to:

- the main subject of the report;
- the scope and purpose of the report;
- the audience who will read it.

The terms of reference should tell you:

- what the report is going to discuss;
- why it is being produced;
- who will read it.

You need to know this information before you begin the process of producing the report:

what? + why? + who? = terms of reference

Title

When you have established the **terms of reference** you can consider the **title**.

For any title to be of value it must:

- reflect the terms of reference;
- be precise and refer directly to the subject of the report.

Main sections/findings

The report will need to be divided into various logical sections and sub-sections. Make full use of **paragraph headings** and **paragraph numbering** including **bullet points**.

This is the section in which you:

- state what you found out;
- clearly present your results, making use of paragraphs, paragraph headings, bullet points, etc.;
- list the essential data. You may want to use tables, graphs and figures.

Use a consistent system of display throughout. Numbered paragraphs might be 1, 2, 3, or 1.1, 1.2, 1.3, etc.

Using effective "signposting" in this way will help the reader pick out elements of the report and will ensure the whole document is easy to follow.

Conclusions

Remember, the purpose of a report is to provide findings and draw conclusions from those findings. This section is vital in a report and allows the key arguments and findings of the report to be drawn together and put into context.

Conclusions need to:

- refer to the purpose of the report;
- state the main points arising in the report;
- be brief and concise.

Recommendations

Any recommendations you make must be presented clearly and follow logically from the conclusions.

This section might, for example, suggest a preferred option from several that were under consideration, make new proposals or recommend further research or investigation.

Bibliography

List all the sources that you have referred to in the main sections of the report. (*See page 97, Writing a Bibliography.*)

A sample title page of a report

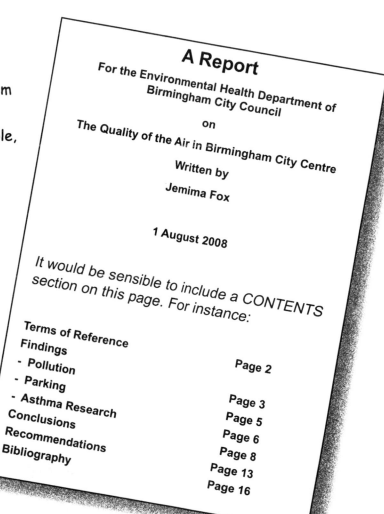

A Report

For the Environmental Health Department of Birmingham City Council

on

The Quality of the Air in Birmingham City Centre

Written by

Jemima Fox

1 August 2008

It would be sensible to include a CONTENTS section on this page. For instance:

The Report's Content

Terms of reference

Report on "The Quality of the Air in Birmingham City Centre" for the Environmental Health Department of the City Council, in order that it can consider possible traffic limiting proposals in the City Centre during peak weekday periods.

Title

The Quality of the Air in Birmingham City Centre

Findings

This report was requested by *(person(s))* in order that *(what the persons are going to do with the report findings).*

In order to produce this report it was necessary to conduct research into the following topics:

....

....

....

and the sources consulted are listed separately in the Bibliography on page X.

1   Pollution.

Make an opening statement about the topic and its relevance to the report then separate into sub-headings, which may, or may not, be numbered.

1.1   UK city average pollution figures.

1.2   City pollution figures related to increase in the number of asthma sufferers.

1.3   etc., etc., etc.

2   Parking.

Conclusions

The purpose of this report was to .... As can be understood from the information contained in "Findings", there is overwhelming evidence that the City of Birmingham's city centre has the second highest pollution figures in the UK............... etc., etc., etc.

Go on to summarise your findings.

Recommendations

The Environmental Health Committee will consider the content of this report when deciding whether to limit traffic in the City Centre during peak periods of the week.

In view of the evidence, the recommendations to the Committee are as follows:

Describe the recommendations, making use of paragraphs, paragraph headings, bullet points, underlined headings, emboldened text, etc.

A report is a business document so you must sign it at the end.

Bibliography

List the documents you consulted in your research here.

Writing a Bibliography

A **bibliography** is a list of sources you have consulted and used information from, for such documents as a report, essay or presentation.

The bibliography is usually produced as an **Appendix** and the information is displayed in categories (books, reference books, newspaper articles and web sites). Each **category heading** appears in alphabetical order, and under each **category heading** the sources are arranged alphabetically. (*See Example 1 below.*)

Example 1

Bibliography

Books

Anderson, M, 2005, *The History of Needlework*, Swan & Signet Books, Preston.

Connaught, J P, 2001, *British Needlework Explained*, Mercantile Books, Edinburgh.

Newspaper Articles

Silvester, C, 2003, 'UK Needlework Trends Since 1851', *The Nottingham Gazette*, 7 April 2003, p15.

Uxbridge, K, 2004, 'Needles and Threads', *The Cornish Messenger*, 20 September 2004, pp49 and 50.

Reference Books

The Encyclopedia of European Embroidery, 2002, 3rd edition, Stitch-in-Time Publishing, Worcester.

Threads Galore, 2005, 1st edition, Sharp Publishing, Norwich.

Web Sites

Ruby, J T 2006, The UK Needlework Association, Nottingham, viewed 24 August 2006 www.uk-nan.org.uk.

Westward, H and Prentice, B 2005, Simply Needlework, Colchester, viewed 25 August 2006 www.simplyneedlework.com.

There is a recommended **list** of information that should be included in each category, and a recommended **order** in which this information should be presented. Some of this information is separated by a comma and some appears in *italics*.

Books	Newspaper Articles
Author's name, comma, initial(s), comma Date of publication, comma *Title* in italics, comma Publisher, comma City/town of publication (not country), full stop.	Author's name, comma Initial(s), comma Date, comma Title of article in **single quotations (')**, comma *Title of newspaper* in italics, comma Date of publication, comma Page number(s) of the article, full stop.
Reference Books *Title of book* in italics, comma Year, comma Edition, comma Publisher, comma City of publication, full stop.	**Web Sites** Author (person or organisation), comma Date (site created or updated), comma Name of publisher, comma City of the publisher, comma Date you viewed the site URL, full stop.

Writing a CV (Curriculum Vitae) and a Covering Letter

A CV (Curriculum Vitae) is a document that gives a brief account of someone's:

- education;
- qualifications;
- experience; and

is written by a job applicant to give information to a prospective employer (someone to whom the applicant is applying for a job).

It is important to state facts, that is not to tell lies, and to give positive information.

An example of how you might set out your CV and the information you should include is shown on *page 100*.

You must take care with spelling, grammar and punctuation and, if you are not presenting a typewritten CV, you must make sure your writing is clear. It is best to use black ink because the CV may be photocopied by the employer and black ink copies more successfully than any other colour.

Divide the information into sections, each under separate headings. Some are a must, whilst others are only useful if they are relevant to you.

See the suggested headings and layout on *page 100*.

Sample Layout for a CV

PERSONAL DETAILS	
Name	*Include your full name(s).*
Address	*Ideally put each line of your address on a separate line. Don't forget your* **post code**.
Telephone no	*Include the area code if quoting a landline number.*
Date of birth/age	*Expressed as 8th March 1986 rather than 8/3/86.*
	Aged 22.
Nationality	*You might decide not to include this information.*
EDUCATION	
Last school attended and qualifications gained	*1999 – 2004 (name of school)*
	List only the passes – be proud of your achievements.
	2004 – GCSEs:
	English Language *Grade B*
	Mathematics *Grade C*
	Key Skills:
	Application of Number *Level 2*
	Communication *Level 2*
	ICT *Level 1*
	etc., etc., etc.
College attended and qualifications gained	*2004 – 2005 (name of college)*
Non-academic achievements	*Passing your driving test*
	Duke of Edinburgh Award
	etc., etc.
Work experience	*Name of firm(s), dates, job title, responsibilities*
Leisure interests (hobbies)	
Referees	*Include two people's names and addresses if possible –* **however, check with them first that they agree to give you a reference**.

Date (mm/yyyy). **You will need to know when your CV was written because you will be gaining additional qualifications and experience all the time and will want to update it for most job applications.**

100

Covering Letter to Accompany a CV

In this section you will learn how to:

▶ present information/ideas on complex subjects concisely, logically and persuasively (W2.1 and W2.2)

▶ use a range a different styles of writing for different purposes (W2.3)

▶ use a range of sentence structures, including complex sentences (W2.4)

▶ ensure written work has accurate grammar, punctuation and spelling and the meaning is clear (W2.6)

Every time that you send out your CV you will need to send out a cover letter with it, whether you are sending your CV in response to an advertisement or direct to an employer.

A cover letter needs to say a lot more than just: 'Here is my CV!', which is all some people seem to think a cover letter should say.

It needs to tell the person why you are writing to them and outline why you are the ideal candidate for the job. You need to pick out the highlights from your CV that are relevant to the specific application, because most jobs you apply for will require a slightly different emphasis of your skills, qualifications and experience.

When employers receive hundreds of applications for one job it is important to get them to read and consider **your** CV. It is important to show them you have style and are just what they are looking for. A covering letter, clipped neatly to your CV, begins to get you noticed for the **right** reasons.

Points to Remember

✓ Use good quality, plain A4 paper.

✓ Use a fountain pen or a good quality ballpoint – it is acceptable to type your covering letter, but be sure, like on your CV, that spelling, grammar and punctuation is 100% accurate.

✓ Use black ink.

✓ If writing by hand, keep your lines straight – but do not use lined paper.

✓ Use neat and legible handwriting.

✓ Keep a copy of your CV and accompanying letter clipped together.

✓ Use the correct name and address, and the title of the person receiving the letter if you know it.

✓ Use a matching salutation and complimentary close.

12 Hospital Fields
York
YO1 5FW

30 November 2008

Miss M Stubbs
Personnel Manager
Fotherington and Crampton Store plc
2 Coppergate
YORK YO1 1FP

Dear Miss Stubbs

Your vacancy for a junior administrator

The Yorkshire Post 14 November 2008

I have read your advertisement for a junior administrator and I am keen to apply. Please find enclosed my CV with details of referees who have agreed they may be contacted on my behalf.

This would seem an ideal opportunity to combine my interest in computers and my interest in a retailing career, and I believe that I have the qualities and qualifications which your advertisement describes.

I am 17 years of age, I care about my appearance and I am enthusiastic and work well as a team member. Additionally, I have a computer and have done some introductory programming. I am ambitious and enjoy using my initiative and taking responsibility when given the opportunity.

I leave college on 21 November and I would be available to start work immediately afterwards. If you wish to interview me, I would be pleased to attend any day after 4pm or on a Saturday. After I leave college, I would be available for interview at any time.

I hope you will consider me as a candidate for the post.

Yours sincerely

Angelina Santos

Angelina Santos

Enc

The purpose of this letter is to add information that it is not normally possible to include on a CV because the headings can be somewhat limiting.

Another purpose is to further try to convince the reader that the writer is ideal for the job in question. Remember your CV or letter of application should get you invited for an interview. No good if it goes into the bin, you won't get your interview then.

Let's look at what Angelina wanted to add to support the facts on her CV:

1   What has Angelina made clear by including a heading to her letter?

       The reader can see immediately the post applied for. This is important information for the reader because there might not be just one job being advertised at a time, especially when the company is large.

       Angelina has included information about where she saw the post advertised. It is not strictly necessary that this information be included, but it does help a firm to decide which source of advertising was best for them so they can use that source in the future. Some firms do ask you to say where you saw the advertisement so it's a good idea to include it on your accompanying letter.

2   The first paragraph is a good opening and indicates a CV is included.

3   In the second paragraph Angelina is reinforcing the fact that she is interested in the job advertised and giving reasons why she thinks she should be considered.

4   Why do you think she has written the third paragraph?

       She's anxious to include some details that she thinks she will show her experience and interest as being suitable for the job and show her as someone who is ambitious and interested in working hard.

5   The fourth paragraph contains information that someone planning to interview Angelina will be pleased to have. By including this information Angelina has made sure the reader knows when she will be available to start work (if she was appointed) and when she will be available for an interview (which she very clearly hopes she will get).

6   Her final paragraph reinforces how keen she is to be interviewed for the job.

I think the result of this letter is likely to lead to her being invited for the next step of the job application process.

All she needs to do now is read the Interview Tips on the following page and hopefully she'll get the job.

Interview Tips

Your job application form or your CV and covering letter impressed the prospective employer and you have been invited to attend an interview.

Study the following advice.

Arriving

Arrive early for your interview. To make sure you do this, carefully research public transport times/car parking arrangements. Know how long it will take you to walk to the employer's premises from the station, bus stop, car park, etc.

How to Dress

Dress smartly and appropriately – forget about being the height of fashion for the day, and don't overload the jewellery.

Walking into the Interview Room

When called in to your interview, walk confidently into the room.

It is usual to shake hands with the interviewer(s). A firm handshake is important.

Be Friendly

You should always maintain eye contact with the interviewer(s), especially with the person asking the question and with anyone to whom you are directing an answer.

Keep a friendly smile on your face to show your enthusiasm.

Sit up Straight

Sit straight in the chair – don't slouch.

When you are nervous it is sometimes difficult to know what to do with your hands. When sitting, fold them on your lap and keep them still.

Speak Clearly

Speak clearly and slowly. When you are nervous there is a tendency to rush your words. Slow down.

Avoid slang terms and poor grammar, such as "like", "basically", "actually", "absolutely", "er", "no problem", "obviously".

Listening to and Answering Questions

Concentrate carefully on the questions you are asked and make sure you understand the question before you answer it.

If you don't fully understand a question, ask for it to be repeated.

Answer the question then stop talking. Don't go on and on and on with your answer.

You are allowed to think before you answer. However, don't spend too much time thinking.

Remember to direct your answer to the person who asked the question. If there are other people present, glance at them from time to time to include them in what you are saying.

Think in Advance

If you have done your research into the job description and the company well, you should be able to anticipate some of the questions you will be asked. Prepare for these before your interview and know what you will say.

Promote your Positive Achievements

Be honest about your weaknesses but positive about your achievements and strengths.

At the End of the Interview

Stand up and shake hands again, thanking the interviewer(s) for their time.

Walk confidently out of the room.

Some Likely Interview Questions

Think about your responses to the following commonly asked interview questions:

- Tell me about yourself.

- What are your greatest strengths and weaknesses?

- Why do you want to work for us?

- What kind of salary are you looking for?

- What do you know about our company?

- Why should we employ you?

- Where do you see yourself in five years time?

- Do you mind working long hours?

- Tell me what you like best about your present job, and why.

- Tell me what you like least about your present job, and why.

- Tell me about when you have taken any responsibility.

- How do you feel about gaining further qualifications?

Would You Like to Ask Any Questions?

When the interviewer has asked all the questions she/he wishes, you are likely to be asked if you wish to ask any questions. Prepare a few questions in advance.

Of course, your questions depend on what was covered during the interview, but think about the following as possible questions:

- Are there opportunities for progression/promotion?

- Would it be possible for me to go to college to gain further qualifications?

- Would I be expected to wear a uniform?

- Would it be possible to see where I would be working?

Finally, you can ask those all-important questions:

- What is the holiday entitlement?

- What is the salary?

Don't ask the last two questions first – whilst you want to know these things, if the interview has not already given you this information, ask other questions first. You don't want the interviewer to think your only concerns are holidays and money!

Taking Part in a Discussion, Giving a Talk or Making a Presentation

This section is divided into two parts:

1   taking part in a discussion; and

2   giving a talk or making a presentation.

Taking Part in a Discussion

What is the *purpose* of a discussion? It is an opportunity to share and exchange ideas and put forward arguments for and against a topic or idea.

Spend a few moments thinking of the roles you might take in a discussion.

Your role will vary in each discussion. You could be the person who is **encouraging** others to do something, or hoping to change their ideas; your role could be to **support** someone else's ideas or opinions. In any discussion it's important to show you are listening to the contribution of the other people involved.

You must expect to have to prepare for your discussion. This might involve making notes of the things you intend to say, such as your main ideas or arguments. You might have to do some research on a subject you don't know a lot about, or even research a subject that is new to you. This is where your research and reading skills will be important, together with your ability to write a range of documents for different audiences – some who understand the topic, others who know nothing about it.

Being Confident in a Discussion

You must think through your ideas and feelings before you begin. Preparing what you will say, and how you will say it, is the key to being confident.

Your Discussion Checklist

- Make sure you understand what is to be the topic of the discussion, and know what is expected of you in the discussion.

- Jot down your immediate thoughts, ideas and opinions.

- Conduct your research to give you a wider knowledge of the topic.

- Make notes from your research of the new ideas you have found useful, or extra information that will support your existing thoughts and ideas.

- Think about what you will say on the topic. You will usually favour one view, but should be aware that the other people might have different views, so you will need to think what you might say about these different views.

- Organise your ideas so they follow a logical order.

- Make notes of what you will say. Try to keep these mainly to headings so they are easy to *refer to* in the discussion. If you have done your research well, you will *know* your topic and be sufficiently confident to talk around the headings you have made. You will lose the others in the discussion if you read from your notes.

- When you are talking, maintain eye contact with the others present and speak clearly (this usually means slowly).

- Speaking slowly means you give yourself time to think and organise what you say and can think about your responses to questions the others may ask.

How to Show you are Listening

- When you are in an encouraging or supporting role, you will mainly be listening to what others say. *Show* you are listening by looking at the person speaking, perhaps occasionally smiling or nodding. Make notes if you have to, in order to help you remember their main idea, arguments or opinions. You don't have to agree with others but a different opinion does not give you the right to dismiss what they say. Show other people respect at all times.

- Ask questions. Be polite and don't interrupt the person speaking. You are expected to act **reasonably**, which means politely, showing respect for the feelings and values of others.

- As we have decided a discussion is a sharing of ideas, try to make sure *everyone* contributes. Whilst it is not very nice to put someone "on the spot" by asking directly "Martha, what are your ideas?" – you wouldn't like it said to you! – you can help Martha to contribute. Say something like "That's a good point, but we haven't heard Martha's ideas yet, let's give her a chance." This is kinder and suggests her contribution is equally valuable.

- Finally, *the aim* of a discussion is usually to reach an agreement about a topic and decide what to do next. Don't let the discussion go round in circles. Keep reminding everyone of the purpose (e.g. to decide responsibilities for organising the keep fit class, to decide on the arguments for and against teenage smoking and related health damage, etc.). Summarise what has been said/agreed, then move on to the next part of the discussion.

- At the end of the discussion, summarise what has been said or decided and make sure everyone has the opportunity to agree.

> **REMEMBER: You don't have to agree with the opinions of others, but this does not give you the right to dismiss what others say. Show people respect at all times.**

Structuring and Delivering Your Talk or Presentation

The ability to make an oral presentation is an important skill. In today's workplace employees will be required to address colleagues or external groups from time to time, and it is also increasingly common for some job interviews to include an oral presentation.

The Five Main Stages in Preparing for a Talk or Presentation

STAGE 1

Address and answer the main questions related to the topic, i.e. **be clear about the purpose of the talk or presentation.**

STAGE 2

Be clear about your brief, i.e. **work out exactly who is your audience, what they know about the topic already (if anything), and what you intend them to know afterwards.**

STAGE 3

Decide what to include, and what **not** to include.

STAGE 4

Decide how to organise the material.

STAGE 5

Make the structure and sequence **logical.**

Delivering Your Presentation

- ✓ It is preferable to stand when you are speaking unless it is an informal presentation to a small group.

- ✓ Ask your audience if they can see and hear you and any material you may be using (overhead projector slides (OHPs), whiteboards, flipcharts, etc.).

- ✓ Try to use your OHPs or software slides as a prompt so that you do not have to use notes.

- ✓ If you do not feel confident enough to do this, then notes on cards are easy to hold. If you use word-processed notes, use a typeface that you can read easily and a type size of 14 point or more and space them out so that they are easy to see at a glance. **Highlighting** key words helps.

- Do not use technical jargon without being prepared to explain it to your audience. Do not assume your audience is as familiar with your topic as you are.

- Do not speak too fast. Vary your pace and, if your voice is normally quiet, then speak a little louder than usual.

- Keep eye contact with your audience. Include the people on the edges of the group. Eye contact keeps your audience engaged in your presentation. Do not address the projector screen, or read out what appears on the screen - always assume your audience can read!

- Do not fiddle with pens, pointers, etc. when speaking. Do not jangle keys or cash in your pocket. Try to keep still.

- If you are one member of a group making a presentation decide how you are going to divide the presentation up. Who is going to do what? The persons not speaking should sit quietly and still!

Images

Amongst other things, images serve to:

- add interest to what you are saying;

- focus the audience's attention;

- clarify facts;

- help the audience remember what you say.

Never Read it Out!

Nervous speakers often make the mistake of reading from their script or the screen. This tactic results in a head down, zero eye contact, monotonous lecture, not an interesting talk with the speaker engaging the audience's attention and interest.

Of course, you know your topic well, having prepared it well, so now prepare a series of **cues** in the form of notes on cards to prompt you about your topic. Your talk will be based on these cues, not on a script!

Creating an Opener

At the beginning, tell the audience the context of your talk and a brief outline of what you are going to cover.

How do you first secure the attention of the audience?

They will want to know two things:

- that your message is relevant and interesting to them; and
- that you have the presence/credibility necessary to deliver it.

What Openers Can You Use?

Ask a relevant question   "Let me begin by asking you a question ...."

Quote a statistic   "Did you know that X% of people in the UK ...."

Use a relevant quotation

Follow these up with a brief explanation of **who you are** and **what you are going to talk about**, emphasising what members of the audience will gain by listening.

Closing With a Flourish

The close is the equivalent to the conclusion section of a report or a letter – where you draw arguments and facts together.

Remind everyone of the objectives of the talk/presentation, and summarise your key points.

"So before I finish, I'd like to summarise the points we've covered this afternoon ...."

It's Question Time! – Handling Questions

- Allow time at the end of your presentation for questions.
- Tell your audience at the beginning when you want to receive questions, to avoid interruptions. For short, time-limited presentations it is best to leave questions to the end. Otherwise you may not have time to finish your presentation.

SECTION 3

PRACTISING READING, WRITING, SPEAKING AND LISTENING SKILLS

The Three Sections of Functional Skills English

There are **three** sections to the Functional Skills English Level 2 Standards, each of which focuses on a different aspect of communicating.

The focuses are:

Speaking and Listening (SL)

Reading (R)

Writing (W)

As you can see from the diagram below, each focus is linked to either one, or both, of the other two.

Each focus contains information on what has to be achieved by a successful candidate. Your skills will be tested, some of them in an examination (*see page 113*).

The purpose of this section of the book is to offer a range of tasks, linked to various employment sectors, that will help you acquire and practise the skills so you become competent and confident. This competence and confidence will help you pass the examination and also to become a student and an employee who can work independently and effectively.

Functional English: Purposeful Activities

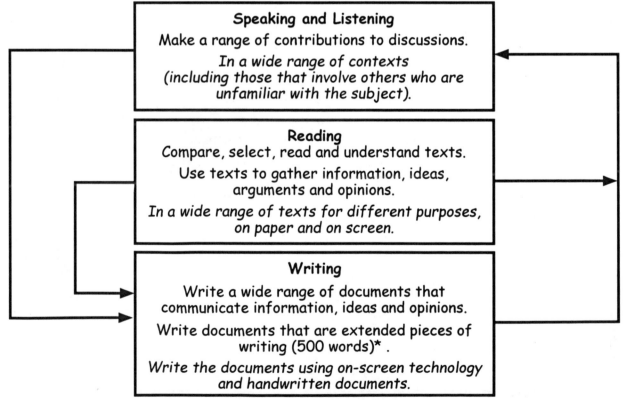

* For the purpose of this book it is assumed the standards will eventually suggest that an 'extended piece of writing' will mean a document containing around 500 words maximum. Not all documents to be written need to be this length.

No focus is done by itself — each focus is linked to another, and each is done for a purpose.

- A document is never read and summarised **without** its content forming part of the **written** document, or the topic of a **discussion/presentation**.

- In order to prepare for a discussion/presentation **(speaking and listening)** there is usually the need for some research, which involves **reading** documents, then notes being **written** to help with the discussion/presentation.

- As a result of a discussion there can be the need to **write** a document or to conduct further research and **read** other documents.

- After a presentation **(speaking)** there is usually an opportunity to **listen** to the questions or comments from the audience.

Employment sectors represented by tasks in this section

Sector of employment	Company name
Art and Design	Creative Images
Call Centres	Ring Ring
Child Care	Bo Peep Nursery
Construction Industry	
Building Company	Another Brick in the Wall
Joinery	Plane Designs
Painting and Decorating	Primary Colours
Plumbing and Electrical	Primary Plumbing
Roofing and Glazing	Primary Cover
Entertainment	Waterside Theatre
Hairdressing	Permanent Waves Hairdressing School
Health and Fitness	First Steps to Fitness
Hotels and Restaurants	Hurchington Manor Hotel and Restaurant
Journalism	Barley Wynd Bugle
Local Government	Brookfield Borough Council
Motor Trade	Triple A Garage
Retail	Sethcote Stationery and Computing Supplies
	Seamless Ladies' Fashion
Small Animal Care	Whiskers and Woofs
Travel	Sunny Destinations Travel

The range of Tasks is designed to provide you with practice for all the Functional English Level 2 content. **However**, as you need to become competent in each of the required areas in Functional English Level 2, your tutor will probably want you to practise tasks from more than just the employment sector in which you are involved, or are interested in following. The examination will be on a general topic, or topics, and this is why Tasks 21, 23, 31, 32 and 33 have been included in this section.

Additionally, when you are involved in work for a **variety of sectors**, you might find it easier to choose a pathway for employment and be interested in having work experience in an area you had not previously considered.

The type of documents and tasks in this book include:

- Completing forms
- Writing memos
- Interpreting graphs, charts and tables
- Writing business letters
- Writing personal letters

- Writing Reports
- Writing a CV and accompanying application letter
- Researching a variety of subjects
- Taking part in discussion
- Making a short presentation

In each task you complete you must pay attention to using correct grammar, spelling and punctuation, and for those tasks that you have handwritten, your writing must be clear and the document neat and tidy.

Task 1: Creative Images - Travel Arrangements

Student Information	Remember
In this task you will complete a telephone message sheet for a member of staff in Creative Images. Ask your tutor for a blank **Telephone Message** sheet.	Telephone messages are brief. *See pages 69 and 70, Taking Messages.* Telephone messages contain only relevant information. The information you include must be accurate. Be clear about dates (don't just put Tuesday of next week). You must be clear in order to avoid any misunderstanding.

Completing a Telephone Message Sheet

Scenario

You work in **Creative Images** and today read details of a recorded telephone message. You will pass on appropriate information to a colleague Zak Black.

Activity

1   In handwriting, taking special care of spelling, grammar and punctuation, complete the telephone message sheet with the details of the call.

These can be found in **Appendix 1**.

Appendix 1

Details of message taken at 11:15 today

"Oh hello, this is a message for Zak Black from Adam Fabianski of Jordison's Gallery, York to confirm our travel arrangements to Prague next week.

I've got the times of the flights from Manchester to Prague, we're going next Tuesday and coming back on the Friday of the same week.   Oh, I'd better leave my contact details - phone number 01904 554790, extension 178.

Anyway, the flight times are Tuesday from Manchester departing 10:05 direct to Prague, flight number TP6772; Friday leaving Prague at 15:50 direct to Manchester. We need to check into Manchester 90 minutes before the departure time. Sorry, I forgot to give the return flight number - it's TP6782.

I tried to get an earlier flight but that would have meant leaving Prague at 08:50, and I know we have an early lunch meeting on Friday so the TP6782 is the best flight for us. I expect it will mean we will be caught up in rush hour traffic in Manchester as we cross to the railway station but it might be all right. Zac Black doesn't know about the early lunch meeting on Friday yet, so I'll give him the timetable of meetings, etc. when I see him at the airport.

Please tell him I will meet him at Terminal 2 on Tuesday at the Avis Car Hire desk. Better make the time 8am and that gives us time to find the check-in desk in the large terminal building because we don't want to be later checking in and miss the flight. We'll have to meet before going to the check-in desk because I have the tickets and will bring them with me on Tuesday. I don't want to risk sending them in the post in case they get lost, then there will be a problem with him getting on the flight. This is an important trip and he must be there.

Just had a thought, the Avis Desk is a long way from the check-in desks, better tell him I'll meet him at the Hertz Car Hire Desk.

Ask him to confirm he has this message and agrees the arrangements. I will be out of the office today after 3pm but he can ring me on my mobile (he's got the number) between 4 and 6 or at home after 6:30. He's got my mobile number but my home number, in case he's lost it, is 01532 345891.

Thank you.

Oh, better tell him we're booked in Tuesday to Thursday night in the Prague Sheraton Hotel.

Bye."

Task 2: Hurchington Manor Hotel – A New Receptionist

Student Information	Remember
In this task you will write a memo from notes left for you by the office manager of Hurchington Manor Hotel and Restaurant.	Display the information in a way that is easy for the reader to interpret.
	Make sure the information you include is accurate.
	Be consistent when you display the times.
	You must sign the memo.
Ask your tutor for a blank **Hurchington Manor Hotel** memo sheet.	*See pages 65 – 68, Writing and Setting out Memos.*

Writing a Memo

Scenario

The office manager of **Hurchington Manor Hotel and Restaurant**, Tomasina Dudka, has asked you to prepare a memo to all the staff so that they know about the appointment of a new receptionist who is replacing someone leaving the company.

Activities

1   Read the note shown below from Tomasina Dudka.

> A NOTE FROM: TOMASINA DUDKA, OFFICE MANAGER
>
> Please send a memo to all staff informing them of the appointment of a new part-time receptionist. Fiona West will begin work on the first Tuesday of next month (give the date please).
>
> Her extension number will be 4180 and she's replacing Barbara Barker who leaves on Friday of this week (supply the date).
>
> Fiona will work Tuesday, Wednesday and Friday mornings each week from 0830 to 1 pm.
>
> Sorry this is a bit muddled, I am in a hurry, tidy it up please.

2   Write the memo from yourself and use the heading **New Receptionist - Fiona West**

Task 3: Barley Wynd Bugle - Fire Alarm Tests

Student Information	Remember
In this task you will write a memo using information included in a memo you have received. Ask your tutor for a blank **Barley Wynd Bugle** memo sheet.	Display the information in a way that is easy for the reader to interpret. Arrange the information in a logical order. Make sure the information you include is accurate. You must sign the memo. When a memo is being sent to everyone in a firm it is acceptable to write All Staff in the "To" section. *See pages 65 - 68, Writing and Setting out Memos.*

Writing a Memo

Scenario

You work in the offices of the **Barley Wynd Bugle** and the company's safety officer, Martin McMillan has asked you to write a memo so that all staff know about the change of arrangements related to the testing of the fire alarms.

Activities

1   Read the memo from Martin - shown in **Appendix 1**.

2   Write the memo from yourself and use an appropriate heading.

MEMORANDUM

To: *Student's name*

From: Martin McMillan, Safety Officer

Date: *Today's date*

Re: New arrangements for Fire Alarm Tests

Would you please send a memo to all staff informing them of the change in the arrangements for the fire alarm tests.

The information you need to include is:

- the weekly tests will take place at 11 am each Monday;

- these will start on the first Monday of next month (include the date please);

- the test will take about 5 minutes;

- this is a change to the usual day and time which, as you know, is 9.30 on the second Thursday in each month;

- the building will not need to be evacuated during the tests.

The memo can be from you and you can sign it.

Thank you

Martin

Task 4: Bo Peep Nursery - Travelling by Train

Student Information	Remember
In this task you will write a memo in response to a note from a member of staff. Ask your tutor for a **Bo Peep Nursery** memo sheet.	Display the information in a way that is easy for the reader to interpret. Make sure you sequence the information logically. Make sure the information you include is accurate. You must sign the memo. *See pages 65 – 68, Writing and Setting out Memos.*

Reading a Timetable and Writing a Memo

Scenario

You work in **Bo Peep Nursery** and today have received a memo from the nursery manager, Cathryn Swinton, requesting details of trains she can catch next week.

Activities

1 Read the memo written by Cathryn Swinton - shown in **Appendix 1**.

2 **Appendix 2** is an extract from the Speed Track Rail Company. Consult this to decide upon suitable journeys for Cathryn.

3 Write a memo in reply to Cathryn giving her the information she has requested.

MEMORANDUM

To   *Student*

From   Cathryn Swinton

Date   *15 August 2008*

Re   Train Times from Cheltenham Spa to Derby

I have to travel to Cheltenham and back next Thursday the 24th. I wish to leave around 8 am from the nearest station to my home, which is Derby.

Please give me details of trains I could catch. My meeting will not finish until around 3.30 pm so the earliest train that I could catch for my return would be no earlier than 4 pm. I want to get home as quickly as possible please.

Can you find details for me and put them in a memo.

Thank you

Cathryn

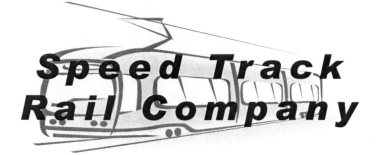

24 AUGUST 2008

FROM
DERBY

TO
CHELTENHAM SPA

RETURN TIMETABLE

No of trains per day	1	2	3	4	5
Dep. station	DBY	DBY	DBY	DBY	DBY
Arr. station	CNMS	CNMS	CNMS	CNMS	CNMS
Departs	08:25	08:38	08:57	09:25	10:38
Arrives	09:49	10:11	10:21	11:10	12:11
No. of changes	0	0	0	1	0
No. of stations the train stops at	4	5	4	6	5
No. of trains per day	1	2	3	4	5
Dep. station	CNMS	CNMS	CNMS	CNMS	CNMS
Arr. station	DBY	DBY	DBY	DBY	DBY
Departs	15:57	16:12	16:18	16:57	17:42
Arrives	17:57	18:38	18:30	18:57	19:11
No. of changes	1	0	0	1	0
No. of stations the train stops at	4	5	3	6	5

Task 5: Brookfield Borough Council – A Conference In Edinburgh

Student Information	Remember
In this task you will write a memo having first conducted some research into train times and hotels. Ask your tutor for a blank **Brookfield Borough Council** memo sheet.	Display the information in a way that is easy for the reader to interpret. Make sure the information you include is accurate. You must sign the memo. *See pages 65 – 68, Writing and Setting out Memos.*

Conducting Research and Writing a Memo

Scenario

You work for **Brookfield Borough Council** and your work involves arranging travel for members of staff when they have to travel in the United Kingdom for the Council.

You have received the Memo from Daniel Godfrey and must provide the information that Daniel has requested.

Activities

1   Read the Memo from Daniel Godfrey - shown in **Appendix 1**.

2   Using appropriate web sites and reference sources, find and print out/ photocopy the required details.

3   Decide upon a suitable hotel.

4   Write a memo including the information that Daniel has asked for.

Include your research documents when you hand this task to your tutor.

BROOKFIELD
BOROUGH
COUNCIL

MEMORANDUM

To: Student's Name

From: Daniel Godfrey

Date: 14 October 2008

Re: Travel Arrangements and Hotel - Edinburgh

I've got to go to Edinburgh next Wednesday to a conference and I'll need to travel up on Tuesday evening, stay in a four-star (4*) hotel in the city and travel back on Wednesday evening after the conference.

Can you find details of

> return train times, and

> hotels in the centre of Edinburgh.

I will want to get to Edinburgh by about 7 pm and leave on the Wednesday at around 4pm if possible.

I'll also want contact details of the hotel you recommend so I can ring them if the train is delayed or I miss it! If possible can you find me a hotel with a pool as I like to swim each evening?

Put all the details you find in a memo to me please.

Thank you.

Daniel

Task 6: Waterside Theatre - A Request for Annual Leave

Student Information	Remember
In this task you will write a memo in response to a note from a member of staff. Ask your tutor for a blank **Waterside Theatre** memo sheet.	Display the information in a way that is easy for the reader to interpret. Make sure the information you include is accurate. You must sign the memo. *See pages 65 - 68, Writing and Setting out Memos.*

Writing a Memo

Scenario

Your work for the personnel manager, Sharon Dale of the **Waterside Theatre**. She has asked you to reply to a memo she has received from Harry Trent.

Activities

1   Read the memo from Harry with the handwritten note by Sharon - shown in **Appendix 1**.

2   Write the memo in reply to Harry, from Sharon.

MEMORANDUM

To   Sharon Dale

From   Harry Trent

Date   13 September 2008

Re   Annual Leave Request

Following the telephone conversation we had this morning, I would like to officially request part of my annual leave this year for 16th to 27th October.

As I mentioned to you, Iris Flowers will be available to cover for me during this leave.

Thank you

Harry

Please reply to Harry, on my behalf (you can send the memo from you and sign it). Say I agree the annual leave request but would like to see both Harry and Iris on 13th October to discuss any outstanding projects that will be handed to Iris in his absence. Suggest 3pm on 13th in my office for the meeting and ask him to bring the files related to the projects to be handed over.

Thank you.

Sharon

Task 7: Primary Colours - Advertising The Company

Student Information	Remember
In this task you will work with a partner to design an advertisement. Ask your tutor for a blank copy of the **Working with a Partner pro forma**.	Make notes of the discussion you have with your partner on the form provided. Use the notes to design the advertisement. *See pages 73 - 75, Writing Advertisements.*

Working With a Partner, Designing a Newspaper Advertisement

Scenario

You work for Primary Colours, a Painting and Decorating company, and have to design an advertisement giving details of the company's services. The purpose of the advertisement will be to eventually put it in the local newspaper to attract custom.

Activities

1   Before you can complete this task, you and your partner will need to show you are clear about the objectives of the task and what you want to include in the advertisement. For this purpose you will need to complete the Working with a Partner pro forma. First read through the task requirements so you know what you have to do.

The information to be included in the advertisement is as follows:

Telephone number: 01633 3467110

Partners: Paul Conway and Peter Campion

Outdoor and indoor painting and decorating undertaken

Wallpapering a speciality

High quality materials - only Soliflex paint is used

Free estimates, with visits at times to suit customers

Business has been established for nine years

No job too small or large, easy or complicated.

2   Design an advertisement suitable for a local newspaper. You are advised to study a local newspaper so you have some ideas of what such advertisements look like and what looks attractive.

3   Take a photocopy, or print out two copies, of the advertisement you design so you each have a copy.

Keep your copy as you will need it in Task 10.

Task 8: Another Brick In The Wall - Quarterly Sales Figures

Student Information	Remember
In this task you will interpret information presented in charts and tables and complete a form to reflect the information.	Make sure the information you enter on the form is accurate.
	Your handwriting should be easy to read.
	Sign the form and date it with today's date.
Ask your tutor for the blank **Quarterly Sales** sheet. An example of this document is shown in **Appendix 2.**	*See pages 60 and 61, Completing Forms.*

Interpreting Information and Completing a Form

Scenario
You work for **Another Brick in the Wall** group of construction companies and have received a note from Simon Kent, the Finance Manager, that you must respond to.

Activities

1   Read the note from Simon Kent. The charts and tables he refers to
     are shown in **Appendix 1**.

> Can
> you please illustrate
>   the information shown in the charts
> and tables on the Quarterly Sales
>   sheet.
>
>   I'll be out of the office until
> tomorrow, so please
>   have this ready for my return.
>
> You can sign and date it today.
>
> Thank you
>
>   Simon

2   Complete the form - **ask your tutor for a blank form** - with the
     information Simon wants.

     Be careful to read the **Explanation of the Data** carefully, so you
     understand what you are to calculate, **then** complete the Quarterly
     Sales sheet.

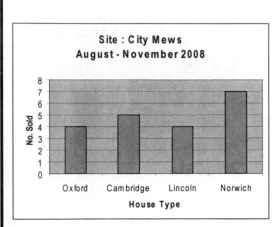

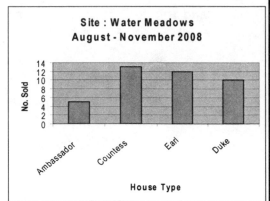

House Type	Price	Number Built
Cambridge	£150,000	15
Lincoln	£125,000	20
Norwich	£160,000	9
Oxford	£225,000	7

House Type	Price	Number Built
Ambassador	£205,000	11
Countess	£195,000	18
Duke	£225,000	15
Earl	£175,000	16

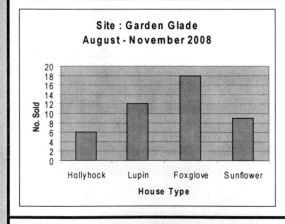

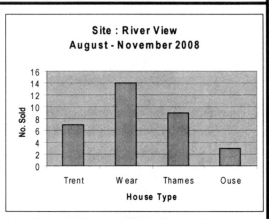

House Type	Price	Number Built
Foxglove	£235,000	24
Hollyhock	£285,000	10
Lupin	£245,000	15
Sunflower	£300,000	11

House Type	Price	Number Built
Ouse	£300,000	6
Thames	£255,000	10
Trent	£200,000	15
Wear	£225,000	28

Appendix 2

Leaders in the construction industry

ANOTHER BRICK IN THE WALL

group of companies

Winner of the 2005-2006 "Best New Homes" Trophy

QUARTERLY REPORT
SALES FIGURES
25 AUGUST TO 25 NOVEMBER 2008

Explanation of the data:

The following information shows, on each site, the house type that has the least number to sell in relation to the number built on the site.

Site Name	House Type	Number Built on Site	Number Yet to Sell as at 25 November 2008

Signed .... Date ....

Task 9: First Steps To Fitness - Applying To Join A Health Club

Student Information	Remember
In this task you will read information and complete a form. Ask your tutor for the blank **Application Form**.	Make sure the information you enter on the form is accurate. Your handwriting should be easy to read. Sign the form and date it with today's date. *See pages 60 and 61, Completing Forms.*

Interpreting Information and Completing a Form

Scenario

You have decided to join the local health club, **First Steps to Fitness,** and today have to complete their application form.

Activities

1   Read each section of the form so you know what information is requested, **together with** the information contained in the 'Details' section below.

2   Ask your tutor for a blank copy of the application form. An example of the form is shown on *page 133.*

3   Sign and date the completed form.

Details

Use your name, but make up an address and contact details.

You want your membership to begin on 1st of next month (be specific) and want to try the club for six months.

You are most interested in the swimming pool, the steam room and the racquet halls, occasionally you may have an interest in the gym and you plan to pay by debit card.

FIRST STEPS TO FITNESS HEALTH CLUB

ALDERLEY ROAD   PEVENSEY GREEN

SUSSEX   SX4 9JZ

☎ 01533 670082   WWW.FSTF.HEALTH.COM

APPLICATION FOR MEMBERSHIP

Name ....Mr/Mrs/Miss/Ms (delete as necessary)

Address

Telephone Number: ....

Mobile: ....   Email address:...

Date Membership to begin:

MEMBERSHIP PLAN

Select choice of Membership from the options below:

Annual	£250	☐	Half-year	£150	☐
Monthly	£40	☐	Family Membership	£200	☐

AREA(S) MOST LIKELY TO BE USED

Gym	☐	Dance Studio	☐	Swimming Pool	☐	Racquet Halls	☐
Steam Room	☐	Sauna	☐	Health and Beauty Area	☐		
Weight Training	☐						

METHOD OF PAYMENT

I wish to pay for the .... Membership at a cost of £ ....

by (tick one box from the options below)

Cheque	☐	Credit Card	☐	Visa/Mastercard	☐
Debit Card	☐	Standing Order	☐	Direct Debit	☐

and will arrange authorisation when I hand in my Application for Membership Form.

Signed .... Date ....

Task 10: Primary Colours - Arranging An Advertisement

Student Information	Remember
In this task you will use the advertisement you produced with a partner in **Task 7** to complete an advertising booking form, and example of which is shown in **Appendix 1**. Ask your tutor for the blank **Advertising Form**.	Make sure the information you enter on the form is accurate. Your handwriting should be easy to read. Sign the form and date it with today's date. *See pages 60 and 61, Completing Forms.*

Referring to Information Produced in Task 7 and Completing a Form

Scenario

In Task 7 you prepared the advertisement for **Primary Colours**. Now you are going to complete an advertising form with the information in your advertisement.

Activities

1   Refer to your original advertisement, reducing the wording if you think it is necessary.

You are advised to **draft** your advertisement first because if you have too many words you **will** need to amend it.

2   Complete the advertising form with your final advertisement. An example of this form is shown in **Appendix 1**.

Note the following information you need:

Primary Colours' address is Jonquil House, 16 Market Lane, YOUR TOWN, Somerset, ST7 2NJ.

The contact telephone number is 01633 3467110 - the fax number is the same.

The advertisement is to be placed in the paper on Wednesday to Friday (inclusive) the week after next and to be a quarter-page spread in colour.

Make sure the form is neatly and clearly completed **and keep it safely as you will be using it in Task 13.**

BARLEY WYND BUGLE

Sycamore Print Works
Cornfield Road, Barley Wynd, Somerset
ST3 4DQ
01455 4762201

Use this form to write the advertisement you wish to appear in the newspaper.

One word/telephone number per box. Please print clearly.

TOTAL NUMBER OF WORDS

NAME AND ADDRESS

DAYTIME TELEPHONE AND FAX NUMBERS

ADVERTISEMENT TYPE

DATE(S) OF INSERTIONS

TOTAL NUMBER OF INSERTIONS

Signature .... Date ....

Task 11: Hurchington Manor Hotel - A Reservation Request

Student Information	Remember
In this task you will write a business letter in response to one enquiring about a possible booking.	A business letter is a formal document.
	See pages 76 - 83, Writing and Setting out Business Letters.
Ask your tutor for a blank **Hurchington Manor Hotel** letterheading.	Make sure your letter contains the following:
	• the date it was written;
	• the name and address of the recipient;
	• a salutation;
	• a complimentary close that matches the salutation;
	• the name of the person who wrote the letter and her title.
	Include only relevant information and make sure the tone is appropriate - in this case **welcoming**.

Writing a Business Letter

Scenario

The hotel's manager - Sally Pitman - has asked you to reply to the letter she received this morning.

Activities

1   Read the letter - **Appendix 1** - from a potential guest.

2   Write the letter, which Sally will sign, so make sure her name and title are used, and include the following information:

-   A double room, with en suite, is available for the nights requested.
-   The charge for the room and breakfast is £73.90 Per night.
-   The room overlooks the hotel's gardens and lake.
-   A table in "the rafters" dining room has been reserved for the dates requested.
-   Dinner is served from 19:30 until 21:30.
-   The cost of dinner varies according to what is chosen on the menu so a menu representing a typical meal is enclosed.

- the hotel's brochure is enclosed.
- be polite and say you are looking forward to welcoming them to your hotel and if there is anything further they wish to know they should not hesitate to write or telephone.

Appendix 1

Black Swan Cottage
Blacksmith's Lane
ALLERTON
Your Town
HP12 5BK

Letter dated 3 days ago

The Manager
Hurchington Manor Hotel
Bridge Road
Bexhill on Sea
Sussex   SE14 6NU

Dear Sir or Madam

ACCOMMODATION 15 - 18 SEPTEMBER

I write to enquire if you have available a double room with bathroom for the nights of 15 – 18 (next month) when my husband and I will be visiting relatives in the area? They have recommended your hotel to us.

I anticipate that we will arrive around 3 pm on the 15th and we will require dinner on the nights of 15th and 17th.

Would you be so kind as to confirm if you are able to accept our booking and, if this is possible, forward to us a hotel brochure together with accommodation and meal rates.

I look forward to hearing from you.

Yours faithfully

Lauren Smedley

Lauren Smedley (Mrs)

Task 12: Creative Images - An Art Exhibition

Student Information

In this task you will write a business letter in response to an incoming one which asks for details.

Ask your tutor for a blank **Creative Images** letterheading.

Remember

A business letter is a formal document.

See pages 76 - 83, Writing and Setting out Business Letters.

Make sure your letter contains the following:

- the date it was written;
- the name and address of the recipient;
- a salutation;
- a complimentary close that matches the salutation;
- the name of the person who wrote the letter and his title.

Make sure the tone of your letter is appropriate and all the information you include is accurate.

Writing a Business Letter

Scenario

You work in **Creative Images Design Gallery**, and the manager, **Matt Barnes**, has asked you to reply to the letter received this morning from Carter Prentice.

Activities

1   Read the letter from Carter Prentice - shown in **Appendix 1** - the purpose of which is to confirm arrangements for an art exhibition the gallery is holding on behalf of Creative Images.

2   Write the letter, which Matt will sign, so make sure his name and title are used and include the following information:

the Artists are: Robb Latham; Marina Tobias and Stephen Harbinson.

the Sculptors are Beth Latham and Caro Fawkes.

The times they will be in the gallery during the exhibition are as follows:

12th : **1000 - 1700** All five will be present all day.

13th: **1000 - 1300** Caro Fawkes, Robb Latham and Marina Tobias.

1300 - 1800 Beth Latham and Stephen Harbinson.

14th: **1000 - 1400** Beth Latham and Caro Fawkes.

1400 - 1800 All five will be present.

Matt will send the database with the names and addresses of those to be invited **no later than 11th November.**

3 You can use "Dear Carter" as the salutation, because the two men know each other. Make sure the complimentary close matches the salutation.

Appendix 1

CONEY ART GALLERY LTD

www.coneyart.paintings.com

8 Finch Street
BAKEWELL
Derbyshire   DB17 4BS   01373 4657890

Letter dated 2 days ago

Mr Matt Barns
Studio Manager
Creative Images
Unit 12, Bakewell Mews
MATLOCK
Derbyshire   DB4 6XW

Dear Matt

Art Exhibition - 12 - 14 December

Following our telephone conversation yesterday, I confirm the arrangements that we discussed.

- The exhibition will take place in our gallery on 12 - 14 December, daily 10:00 to 18:00.
- On the first day there will be an Artists' Reception at 16:00.
- On the 14 December from 17:00 until the close at 18:00, the paintings and sculptures will be offered for sale.

I wonder if you could now answer these questions?

1 At what times, and on which days, will the artists be in the gallery?
2 When will you provide me with the details of who you wish to invite to the Artists' Reception on 12 December?

I look forward to hearing from you and thank you for having your exhibition at our gallery.

Yours sincerely

Carter Prentice
Gallery Director

Task 13: Primary Colours - Placing An Advertisement

Student Information	Remember
In this task you will write a business letter requesting advertising space in a local newspaper. Ask your tutor for a blank **Primary Colours** letterheading.	A business letter is a formal document. *See pages 76 - 83, Writing and Setting out Business Letters.* Make sure your letter contains the following: • the date it was written; • the name and address of the recipient; • a salutation; • a complimentary close that matches the salutation; • the name of the person who wrote the letter and his title. Make sure the tone of your letter is appropriate and all the information you include is accurate.

Writing a Business Letter

Scenario

In Task 10 you completed an advertising form. Now you must write to the advertising manager of the local newspaper - the Barley Wynd Bugle - and arrange for the advertisement to be inserted in their paper.

Activities

1   Write the letter to the Barley Wynd Bugle, which one of your colleagues, Rajput Chowla, the Finance Officer, will sign, so make sure his name and title are used as the person who signs the letter, and include the following additional information:

Ask for the account to be sent to Primary Colours for the attention of Rajput Chowla.

Say that if the advertisement proves to be successful you will want to advertise in a similar way every month for the next three months and ask if there will be any discount available as a returning customer.

Task 14: Primary Plumbing - A Boiler Servicing Contract

Student Information

In this task you will write a business letter in response to one which makes a request.

Ask your tutor for a blank **Primary Plumbing** letterheading.

Remember

Make sure your letter contains the following:

- the date it was written;
- the name and address of the recipient;
- a salutation;
- a complimentary close that matches the salutation;
- the name of the person who wrote the letter and his title.

Make sure the tone of the letter is appropriate (in this case you are trying to gain a customer) and all the information you include is accurate.

Set out the information clearly so the reader is able to understand the information at a glance.

See pages 76 - 83, Writing and Setting out Business Letters.

Replying to a Business Letter

Scenario

Jed Carnforth, service manager of **Primary Plumbing**, has received a letter of enquiry from a potential customer, Allan Allsop. He has asked you to reply to the letter.

Activities

1 Read the letter from Allan Allsop - shown in **Appendix 1**.

2 Write the letter, which Jed Carnforth will sign, adding the information he has included in his note at the bottom of the letter.

Appendix 1
26 Beech Road
Abingfield Village
YOUR TOWN
GH9 2GY
01633 788277

Letter dated 2 days ago

Service Manager
Primary Plumbing
Electrical and Plumbing Contractors
12 Water Lane
YOUR TOWN
GH1 7JF

Dear Sir or Madam

My family and I have recently moved into this home and wish to have the Glowmoth gas boiler serviced as we know the former owners had not had this done in the previous four years.

Would you be interested in arranging an annual service and maintenance contract? If so, would you please send details of your charges and then we can probably arrange for you to carry out the first service, hopefully some time early next month.

Yours faithfully

A Allsop

Allan Allsop

Reply to Mr Allsop please, thanking him for his letter of enquiry. The service contract option details are as follows:

Primary One
Annual maintenance/service   £60.00
Parts and labour cover if needed in the year   £45.00
ANNUAL CHARGE   £105.00
This cover guarantees 24-hour call out and repairs, or parts replacement, within 24 hours.

Primary Two
Annual maintenance/service and parts   £80.00
Labour   £10.00
ANNUAL CHARGE   £90.00

Primary Three
Annual maintenance/service   £50.00
Parts and labour, if required, not included.
ANNUAL CHARGE   £50.00

If Mr Allsop agrees to take out a contract, the earliest we could carry out a service would be the 18th (next month).

We look forward to hearing from him.

Thank you - Jed

Task 15: Primary Cover - A Work Experience Placement

Student Information

In this task you will write a business letter in response to one which makes a request.

Ask your tutor for a blank **Primary Cover** letterheading.

Remember

Make sure your letter contains the following:

- the date it was written;
- the name and address of the recipient;
- a salutation;
- a complimentary close which matches the salutation;
- the name of the person who wrote the letter and his title.

Make sure the tone of the letter is appropriate, and all the information you include is accurate.

Set out the information clearly so the reader is able to understand information at a glance.

See pages 76 - 83, Writing and Setting out Business Letters.

Writing a Business Letter

Scenario

Rupert Stanford is personnel manager of **Primary Cover**, and he has received a letter from the Head of the Department of Construction in a local Community College enquiring if Primary Cover could take a construction student on work experience. You have to write the letter for Rupert to sign.

Activities

1 Read the letter from Patrick Texas - shown in **Appendix 1**.
2 Write the letter, which Rupert Stanford will sign, agreeing to the dates mentioned.

Additional Information

3   Mention you are not certain at the moment where Jack will be based but this is likely to be at the River View Development in Connelton Village, being developed by the parent company Another Brick in the Wall. It is a site of 59 detached homes and work began there last month, with the second phase due to begin the month after next.

4   Ask if Jack can come in to meet company members and the construction site manager (Aidan Simplinski) on the 14th of next month (be specific please) at 11:00.

Appendix 1

 Ward Nelson Community College
Pinewood Road   YOUR TOWN
GH7 11SQ

www.wardnelson.ac.uk
enquiries@wardnelson.co.uk
01633 342398

Letter dated 3 days ago

Mr R Stanford
The Personnel Manager
Primary Cover Roofing Contractors
Studley Court
7 Minnow Road
YOUR TOWN
GH5 5PP

Dear Mr Stanford

<u>WORK EXPERIENCE REQUEST FOR JACK MASTERS 12 - 24 FEBRUARY</u>

Following our telephone conversation today, I am pleased to put in writing the request for work experience.

Jack is a year 11 student who is keen to begin a Modern Apprenticeship in June. In order to give him some experience in the construction industry, it would seem sensible if his work experience could be related to the industry.

As your company has very kindly taken some of our students on previous occasions, I wondered if you would be able to offer a two-week opportunity for Jack beginning on 12 February next year?

If, as you indicated on the telephone, this is likely to be possible, could you confirm this starting date is acceptable to you and I will arrange for Jack to visit you. After his visit I will send the necessary forms for you to sign.

I look forward to hearing from you.

Yours sincerely

P Texas

Patrick Texas
Head of the Department of Construction

Task 16: Whiskers and Woofs - A Cattery and Kennels Booking

Student Information	Remember
In this task you will write a business letter in response to an enquiry from a client. Ask your tutor for a blank **Whiskers and Woofs** letterheading.	Make sure your letter contains the following: • the date it was written; • the name and address of the recipient • a salutation; • a complimentary close that matches the salutation; • the name of the person who wrote the letter and her title. Make sure the tone of the letter is welcoming, and that all the information you include is accurate. See pages 76 - 83, Writing and Setting out Business Letters.

Studying Tabular Information and Replying to a Business Letter

Scenario

Florence McFarlane is the manager of **Whiskers and Woofs**, a cattery and kennels. She has received a letter from Tania Mann asking if her cat and dog can be booked into the residency in March. You now have to reply to that letter of enquiry after checking the occupancy chart.

Activities

1 Read the incoming letter - **Appendix 1**.

2 Look at the occupancy chart - **Appendix 2** - and check whether there is a cabin and kennel available in March for the dates in question.

3 If there is accommodation available, write the letter, which Florence McFarlane will sign. Mention the cabin/kennel numbers you will assign to the animals.

4 Include details of the daily rates, which are as follows: cats £6.50 per day; dogs £8.90 per day.

15 Cleveland Avenue
Coquet Village
WEST YORKSHIRE
WR5 1FM

Letter dated yesterday

Mrs F McFarlane
Manager
Whiskers and Woofs
Clifton House
PAWSLEY
West Yorks   PW9 5VC

Dear Mrs McFarlane

My family is off on holiday in March and we will want our dog (Benny) and cat (Magic) to stay with you whilst we are away.

We'd like to bring them on 7 March and collect them on 16 March.

Could you confirm this booking is possible please, together with providing details of your latest daily charges?

Yours sincerely

T Mann

Tania Mann (Mrs)

OCCUPANCY for the month of MARCH

	Cabin/Kennel Number	Dates of Occupancy	Pet's Name
C A T T E R Y	1	6 - 18	Mia
	2	9 - 27	Pickle
	3	16 - 24	Olive
	4	3 - 15	Sam
	5	8- 19	Persia
	6		
	7	14 - 23	Merlin
	8	6 - 9	Montgomery
	9		
	10		
K E N N E L S	1		
	2	3 - 10	Max
	3	11 - 17	Toby
	4	4 - 19	Rufus
	5		
	6	19 - 27	Icer
	7	8 - 19	Jonty
	8		
	9	2 - 10	Bramble
	10	3 - 12	Ivan
	11		
	12		

Task 17: Permanent Waves Hairdressing School - An Educational Visit

Student Information	Remember
In this task you will write a business letter in response to an enquiry **and** a memo to members of staff. Ask your tutor for a blank **Permanent Waves** letterheading and memo sheet.	Make sure your letter contains the following: • the date it was written; • the name and address of the recipient; • a salutation; • a complimentary close that matches the salutation; • the name of the person who wrote the letter and her title. Make sure the letter is welcoming, and that all the information you include is accurate. *See pages 76 - 83, Writing and Setting out Business Letters.* The memo you write must display all the information clearly. Don't forget to sign the memo. If you write a memo to more than one person, put each person's name in the "to" section with each name separated by a comma. *See pages 65 - 68, Writing and Setting out Memos.*

Studying Tabular Information and Replying to a Business Letter and Writing Memos

Scenario
Jane Felsham is the Director of **Permanent Waves Hairdressing School** and has received a request from a local college for a student visit. You have to consult a staff diary and decide who can take part in the visit then write to all parties concerned.

Activities

1 Read the letter from Kay Langley of Ward Nelson Community College, and Jane's comment shown in **Appendix 1**.

2 Check the diary - **Appendix 2** - to see which member(s) of staff could be involved in the activities.

3 When you have decided who will be involved, send them a memo that outlines their involvement in the visit. Remember to give them the background, i.e. who is visiting, from where, how many there will be in the party, what they will have to do with the visitors, the times, the name of the member of staff accompanying the party, etc. You can send the same memo to each member of staff. In this way, each will know the involvement of the other person.

4 Reply to the letter from Kay Langley - Jane will sign it so write it in her name - and give details of the arrangements you have made. Mention the name(s) of the staff involved, the session times and details. Make the letter welcoming - the college do supply you with students each year so the visit is important.

U.S. Air Force photo by Airman 1st Class Cassandra Jones

Appendix 1

Ward Nelson Community College
Pinewood Road   YOUR TOWN
GH7 11SQ

www.wardnelson.ac.uk
enquiries@wardnelson.co.uk
01633 342398

Letter dated yesterday

Mrs Jane Felsham
Director
Permanent Waves Hairdressing School
Floor 4 Tavistock Building
Westcliffe Road
YOUR TOWN
GH7 3BL

Dear Mrs Felsham

<u>STUDENT VISIT - 24 FEBRUARY</u>

In previous years Permanent Waves Hairdressing School has very kindly allowed a small group of students who are interested in progressing in their hair and beauty career to have a half-day visit to your organisation.

I wonder if you would be able to offer a similar visit for six of our current students on 24 February, at a time to suit yourselves? The six students would be accompanied by Susan Hartley, their Group Tutor.

I look forward to hearing from you in due course.

Yours sincerely

Kay Langley

Kay Langley
Head of the Department of Hair and Beauty

Kay's correct - we do offer this college a visit once a year.

Please look at the commitments of the staff in the diary and see who can get involved. The timetable would be:

Arrive here 1030 - greeted by whoever is free and who can then give them a short tour of the facilities until 1100. 1100-1230 presentation by a member of staff about the work of the school and its successes in the hair and beauty industry. Questions by the students. End of visit at 1250.

You might have to involve two members of staff, and if you do, you need only send one memo, addressed to both people, giving details of the arrangements in which they are both involved. Also write back to Kay to give her the information. Say we are all looking forward to welcoming her students again, etc.

Thank you. I'll sign the letter, you can sign the memo(s).

Jane

Diary   24 February

	Kay Prentice	Salfri Gupta	Maria Boruc	Sylvia Cullin	Toni Greene	Agnes Fastnet
0900	▓		▓			
0930	▓	▓			▓	
1000		▓			▓	
1030					▓	
1100	▓			▓		
1130	▓					▓
1200	▓		▓			
1230						
1300						
1330		▓				
1400		▓	▓			
1430		▓	▓			
1500			▓	▓		▓
1530				▓		▓
1600					▓	
1630						
1700	STAFF MEETING HOUR					
1730						

Shaded boxes indicate times when staff have appointments and are unavailable.

Task 18: Triple "A" Garage - Car Service Bookings

Student Information	Remember
In this task you will complete a form.	Make sure the information you enter on the form is accurate.
You will also take the part of the garage's workshop reception manager and telephone a customer.	Your handwriting should be easy to read.
	See pages 60 and 61, Completing Forms.
Ask your tutor for the blank **Triple "A" Workshop Booking** sheets.	Make notes of what you will say before your telephone call.
	Speak clearly and slowly, introducing yourself and the company you represent at the start of the call.
	See pages 83 and 84, Making Telephone Calls.

Transferring Information onto a Form and Making a Telephone Call

Scenario

Allan A Aston who runs **Triple "A" Garage** has asked you, as the workshop manager, to allocate the work booked into the car workshop next week.

Activities

The cars booked into the workshop, starting on Monday of **next week**, are detailed in **Appendix 1**.

1 Ask your tutor for the blank **Workshop Booking Sheets**. Use a separate one for each day of the week.

2 Book each "job" onto the sheets, allowing each mechanic a 20-minute break after the estimated completion time of the job so that he can complete the necessary paperwork.

Put the entries on the form in **time** order for each day.

3 With your tutor taking the roll of one of Monday's customers, telephone the customer to tell them what time their car is booked in for its service. The customer gave you a choice of times for their vehicle to be serviced and now you have completed the sheet you can confirm the time.

Don't forget to say who you are and where you are calling from. Be polite and make sure what you say is accurate.

Appendix 1

This is an extract from the workshop booking sheet and the first entry has been completed as an example:

Date and Booking In Time	Car Reg. No	Make and Model	Owner's Name	Mechanic
Monday (and date) 0800	SV57 ODG	Vauxhall Astra	Mr Blandy	Seth

<u>Monday's date - Mechanics Seth, Stan, Alex, Keith, Neil</u>

<u>(Neil specialises in Citroens and this make is to be booked to him)</u>

0800   Mechanic: Seth   Mr Blandy's Vauxhall Astra SV57 ODG   (1 hour)

0830   NU06 HMX   Miss Trotter's Toyota Yaris   (90 minutes)

0845   Dr Hutchinson's Renault Clio   NE56 XRJ   (45 minutes)

0930   Mrs Potter's Toyota Land Cruiser   YB51 YYP   (2 hours)

1115   Ford Focus BE53 HLV   Mr Painter   (90 minutes)

1050   Mr Hopper Citroen C3   HB05 TTZ   (2 hours)

1255   NV04 TYN Vauxhall Corsa   Mr Stokes   (3 hours)

1305   Saab 90   Miss Kapur   DK 119B   (1 hour)

1315   Ford Galaxy   Mrs Gold   DG06 MDG   (40 minutes)

<u>Tuesday's date - Mechanics Alex, Keith, Neil and Seth</u>

0900   Mr Jacobs   SW04 TBF   Ford Fiesta   (3 hours)

1130   Renault Clio   MN02 NGN   Miss Gupta   (90 minutes)

1030   Dr Pentland   Toyota Jazz BT57 JJS   (2 hours)

1400   Mr Hardwick   SP55 WPK   Citroen C4   (90 minutes)

1050   Mr Unwin TB06 YHY   Citroen C2   (60 minutes)

Task 19: Seamless Ladies' Fashions - Placing An Order

Student Information	Remember
In this task you will complete an order form.	Make notes of what you will say before your telephone call.
Before you complete the form you will have to telephone the supplier to query details about one item.	Speak clearly and slowly, introducing yourself and the company you represent at the start of the call.
	See pages 83 and 84, Making Telephone Calls.
Ask your tutor for the blank **Purchase Order Form**.	Make sure the information you enter on the form is accurate.
	Your handwriting should be easy to read.
	See pages 60 and 61, Completing Forms.

Making a Telephone Call and Completing an Order Form

Scenario

Celestra (Esta) Byrne is the owner of **Seamless Ladies' Fashions** and wants to place an order for some fashion garments for next season. She is uncertain about one item in the catalogue and has asked you to telephone the supplier then complete her purchase order form.

Activities

1 Read the note from Esta - **Appendix 1**. It lists what to order and gives details of the question she wants you to ask the supplier.

2 Make notes of what you will say and make the phone call, with your tutor taking the part of someone in the Sales Department of Betta Fashions Direct.

3 Complete the order form with the information supplied by Betta Fashions Direct and also taking into account the comments in Esta's note. An example of the order form is shown in **Appendix 2**.

Order to Betta Fashions Direct: Eskdale Manufacturing Park, Factory 3, Clement Road, Leeds, W Yorks SW0 8FE   Date it today.

Cotton Skirt - Gypsy Trim

| 4 Size 12 | Yellow and Red | £6.00 each | Cat. No. GT5608 |
| 6 Size 12 | Green and Orange | £6.00 each | Cat. No. GT5611 |

Cotton Waistcoat

| 10 Size 10 | Grey/White Stripe | £7.00 | Cat. No. CW4443 |

Cotton Trouser

| 4 Size 8 | White | £12.00 | Cat. No. CT2288 |
| 6 Size 14 | Black | £14.00 | Cat. No. CT2359 |

Polyester Waistcoat

| 10 Size 14 | White | £20.00 | Cat. No. PW0894 |
| 10 Size 12 | Grey | £20.00 | Cat. No. PW0992 |

Linen Cropped Jacket

| 4 Size 8 | Sand | £30.00 | Cat. No. LJ3349 |
| 4 Size 12 | Red | £30.00 | Cat. No. LJ5562 |

I'd like to order three of the **Linen Cropped Jacket size 14**, but there is no catalogue number, colours or price. Can you ring **Betta Fashions Direct** to find out this information please, then add this to the order. If they do grey in this size I'd like grey please.

Delivery is **48-hour express delivery service.** There are no special instructions. Calculate totals for each item ordered **and** the order's total.

Thank you
Esta

Appendix 2

Seamless Ladies' Fashion

15 Perth Street NEWBRIDGE
Warwickshire WK8 4FR
Telephone: 01622 7626512

PURCHASE ORDER
NUMBER: BFD 191/00

ORDER DATE:

Delivery Address   15 Perth Street, NEWBRIDGE, Warwickshire   WK8 4FR

DELIVERY METHOD	SPECIAL INSTRUCTIONS				
QTY	CATALOGUE NUMBER	DESCRIPTION	SIZE	UNIT PRICE	ITEM TOTAL
Order to:				TOTAL	

Task 20: Bo Peep Nursery – New Starters In The Crèche

Student Information	Remember
In this task you will complete a form and write a memo.	Make sure the information you enter on the form is accurate.
Ask your tutor for the blank **New Starters** form and a **Bo Peep** memo sheet.	Your handwriting should be easy to read.
	See pages 60 and 61, Completing Forms.
	You must sign the memo as its writer.
	See pages 65 - 68, Writing and Setting out Memos.

Completing a Form and Writing a Memo

Scenario

Cathryn Swinton of **Bo Peep Nursery** wants you to complete a form that will show the details of the children new to the nursery who are within a certain age group.

Activities

1. Read the note from Cathryn - **Appendix 1**.
2. Transfer the information from Cathryn's database on to the form your tutor will give you.
3. Make sure your writing is neat and you have spelt all the names correctly.
4. Write a short memo to Cathryn attaching the completed form.

Appendix 1

NOTE FROM

CATHRYN SWINTON

Below is the extract I have printed from my database showing those children who are new to the nursery and starting with us on Monday of next week.

Will you complete the form that indicates starters in the crèche. You will remember the children in the crèche are those up to, and including, 1 year and 11 months of age.

We usually enter the information on these forms in alphabetical order of surname. **Please note I have entered one set of details incorrectly, "Breeze, Gail" should have been entered as "Gail Breeze" (Breeze is the surname).**

Child's Name	Age	Adult to Contact	Contact Number	Day	am or pm
Louis Trent	8 months	Terri Trent	5766381	Wed	pm
				Thurs	am & pm
Fariq Sandip	14 months	Reena Abaloni	776756433	Tues	am & pm
				Thurs	pm
				Fri	am & pm
Colette Spinner	5 months	Jayne Spinner	5782291	Mon to Thurs	pm
Breeze, Gail	11 months	Anne Breeze	778936542	Tues & Thurs	am
				Mon	pm
Seth Black	23 months	Peter Browne	5537001	Wed	pm
				Thurs	am
Jade Green	17 months	Patty Black	753890021	Mon & Tues	am
				Wed & Fri	pm
				Thurs	am & pm
Eliza Coombes	35 months	Lourdes Clyde	799546433	Monday	am & pm
				Friday	am
Fern Justice	21 months	Stan Justice	5566906	Mon to Wed	am & pm
Amber Grace	13 months	Connie Benson	746773997	Mon	pm
				Tues	pm
				Wed	am & pm
Charity Inglis	28 months	Karen Spinks	5620025	Mon	pm
				Thurs	am & pm
				Fri	pm
Abbra Khan	21 months	Lillian Khan	5505237	Tues & Wed	am & pm
Jamil Chawla	23 months	Mukesh Chawla	74545477	Mon	pm
				Tues	am
				Wed	am & pm

Thank you

Cathryn

Task 21: Personal Interest - Providing a Friend with Information

Student Information

In this task you will write a personal letter to a friend telling them you have joined a fitness club.

You will need to refer to the **Application Form** you completed in Task 9.

Remember

A personal letter is written from someone's home address to either an individual person (a friend perhaps), or a company.

See pages 87 - 92, Writing and Setting Out Personal Letters.

Spelling, grammar and punctuation are still important in a personal letter.

Remember to sign the letter.

Writing a Personal Letter

Scenario

You have recently been speaking to a friend who lives near you and this friend has expressed an interest in learning about the fitness club you have just joined and perhaps becoming a member. You are going to write to your friend giving details you think might be of interest.

Activities

Write a personal letter to your friend. *You can use a fictitious addresses for yourself and your friend.*

1 The letter is **informal** but contains facts you think might be of interest. For instance, the fees and the facilities offered and other information that you consider to be relevant for someone thinking of joining.

You can use the complimentary close "Kind regards", if you wish.

Task 22: Ring Ring - Target Details

Student Information	Remember
In this task you will interpret a chart and display the information in the form of a table.	You are displaying information in a different format because not everyone is able to, easily and accurately, interpret graphical information.
You will also write a memo.	Display the information in a way that is easy for the reader to interpret. It is usual, when displaying names, to place the **surname** first.
Ask your tutor for copies of the blank **Target Results** form and the **Ring Ring** memo sheet.	In **both** documents, make sure you sequence the information logically and that all the information you give is accurate.
	You must sign the memo.
	See pages 65 - 68, Writing and Setting out Memos.

Interpreting a Chart and Writing Memos

Scenario

Ring Ring Call Centre operates a telephone-based answering service for 50 companies in the United Kingdom. It is based in Bristol and has 300 members of staff who are assigned to various teams, each with a team leader.

On a monthly basis, performance targets, set by the client company, are monitored for each team.

Activities

Appendix 1 gives details, in the form of a bar chart, of the performance figures related to the speed of answering a call for the client company Wrightson Insurance plc, **last month**.

1   The section manager in charge of the Wrightson account - Trinny Ringwood - wants you to display the findings of the graph in tabular form in the format shown in **Appendix 2. Note** that the information for **Team A** has been included for your guidance. Be consistent in the display of the remaining information.

2   As a result of this analysis and transfer of data, Trinny wants you write a memo to the team leaders who head the team(s) which **met** the target.

<u>Note</u>

The memo can be addressed to a number of people. The names should be separated by commas and be written on one line.

You know Trinny's title. Date the memo today.

The **purpose** of the memo is to congratulate the team leaders in meeting the performance targets for Wrightson Insurance plc (mention the month in question). Give them information on their highest individual target percentages.

Finish with a few words of encouragement for future months (Trinny hopes they will remain in this category and if this month's figures reflect this, each team member will receive a 2% bonus at the end of this financial year in March).

Appendix 1

RING RING CALL CENTRE

Client: Wrightson Insurance plc

Agreed targets for call answering service

Target met: minimum of 80% of calls answered within 8 seconds

Target nearly met: minimum of 70% calls answered within 8 seconds

Target failed : 69% and fewer calls answered within 8 seconds

SECTIONS A – F % ANSWERED CALLS (LAST MONTH AND THIS YEAR)

Team	Leader
A	Jannit Jalilla
B	Sara Garritty
C	Pandit Singh
D	Phillippa Tavares
E	Colin Teake
F	Gareth Betts

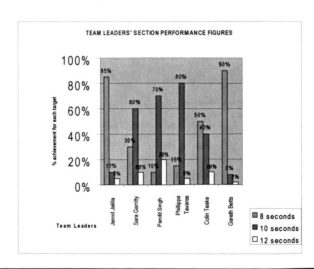

TEAM LEADERS' SECTION PERFORMANCE FIGURES

RING RING CALL CENTRE

Client: Wrightson Insurance plc

Agreed targets for call answering service

Target met: 80% of calls answered within 8 seconds

Target nearly met: 70% calls answered within 8 seconds

Target failed : 69% and lower calls answered within 8 seconds

Month .... 20..

Team	Team Leader	Highest recorded category			
		Result (✓ relevant category)			
		Met	Nearly met	Failed	% figure
A	Jalilla, Jannit	✓			85
B					
C					
D					
E					
F					

SUMMARY

Teams	Met target	Nearly met target	Failed to meet target
TOTAL NO. OF TEAMS FOR EACH TARGET			
Successful Team Leader(s)			
Unsuccessful Team Leader(s)			

Task 23: Personal Interest - Planning a Holiday

Student Information	Remember
In this task you will research information on two Spanish islands and put together fact sheets from your research. You will then write a fax to a friend and another fax to a travel company. Ask your tutor for copies of the blank **Fax** form.	A fax is an official document, but it can be seen by anyone who comes across it on the fax machine before it is sent to the person to whom it is addressed. Be careful, therefore, not to be rude or to include confidential information - just treat it like a letter which is delivered more quickly! *See 85 and 86, Sending Faxes.* Include your research documents with the task you hand to your tutor. This might involve taking a photocopy and attaching the copy to your work. Any images you use in your fact sheets must be appropriate and help the reader to understand the topic. *See pages 92 - 98, Writing Reports* and *Writing a Bibliography.*

Conducting Research, Writing Fact Sheets and Faxes

Scenario

You have received a fax from your friend - shown in **Appendix 1**. As a result you carry out some research and prepare two fact sheets. You then prepare two faxes, one to your friend and the other to **Sunny Destinations Travel**.

Activities

1   Read the fax from your friend – **Appendix 1**.

2   Conduct research into the two holiday destinations being considered. You might like, initially to use the internet to view this site: www.balearicsislands.com. You will find other information, possibly from holiday brochures.

Look for images that you can use in your fact sheets on each island destination.

3   Put together an illustrated fact sheet on each island that will include information to help your friends make a decision about which island to

book as a holiday destination. **Each** fact sheet should contain no fewer than **250 words.**

4   Write a fax in reply to your friend telling him you have done the research and produced fact Sheets which you will drop off at his house this evening.

5   Send a fax to **Sunny Destinations Travel – fax number** 01674 555025 – asking them for information on one of the hotels you recommended to your friend.

Student Information   **Appendix 1**

FAX

For: **Student's Name**

Fax number: **01236 459201**

From: **Jeremy**

Fax number: **01236 488201**

Date: **Today's date**

Regarding: **Summer holiday**

Number of pages: **1**

Comments:

Hi. Do you remember Tom and I talked about going to either Formentera or Majorca for a week this coming August?

You said you'd help us make a decision by doing some research into things like temperatures, 2* hotels you recommend, any costs you can find, things to do on the island, etc.

I'm busy at work for the next week so if you have time and could do this research for us it would be great.

Regards J

Task 24: Brookfield Borough Council - The National Blood Service

Student Information	Remember
In this task you will research the work of the National Blood Service and write a report.	Include your research documents with the task you hand to your tutor. It may be that you have to take a photocopy and attach this copy to your work. *See pages 92 - 98, Writing Reports and Writing a Bibliography.*

Conducting Research and Writing a Report

Scenario

Your employer, **Brookfield Borough Council**, is hosting a "Give Blood - Help Save a Life" event on the second Thursday of next month. The aim of holding it on Council premises is to encourage employees to give 45 minutes or so of their time to donate blood.

Your boss - Karen Tidey - has asked you to write a report on the topic, which will then go on the Council's intranet.

Activities

1   Conduct research into the topic. You might want initially to use the internet to view the site www.blood.co.uk, but there will be other information you will find and use.

   Apart from the things you regard as important, your report must contain information on the following:

   - what happens in a blood donation session;

   - who cannot give blood;

   - what makes up blood and how each part is used;

   - the current blood stocks.

2   Put together your report, which must contain no fewer than 500 words, using the headings:

   - Title
   - Findings
   - Conclusions

   Don't forget the aim of the report is to encourage people, especially those who have not done so before, to donate. Don't forget also to sign and date the report.

Task 25: Waterside Theatre - It's Show Time

Student Information	Remember
In this task you will research two shows that your theatre is thinking of staging next season and write a report.	Include your research documents with the task you hand to your tutor. It may be that you have to take a photocopy and attach this copy to your work. *See pages 92 - 98, Writing Reports and Writing a Bibliography.*

Conducting Research and Writing a Report

Scenario

You work for the manager of the **Waterside Theatre**, Barny Penhaligon. He wants you to research two musicals because the theatre is considering staging one of them next season.

Activities

1 Conduct research into two of the following shows - **Mamma Mia; Hairspray and Oliver.**

   Amongst other things you consider to be appropriate you should include details of the following -

   - what the show is about, and

   - the length of the show.

   > Remember you will be writing a report on your findings.

2 Write your report, which will include details of **both** shows and should contain no fewer than 500 words.

   Use the headings:

   - Title

   - Findings

   - Conclusions.

   Sign and date your report.

Task 26: Plane Designs - A Brochure

Student Information	Remember
In this task you will create an illustrated brochure. You will be involved in researching the work of a craftsman joiner.	Include your research documents with the task you hand to your tutor. It may be that you have to take a photocopy and attach this copy to your work.
	Any images you use must be appropriate and help the reader to understand the topic.
	You are producing an advertising brochure.
	See pages 73 - 75, Writing Advertisements.

Conducting Research and Producing a Brochure

Scenario

Peter Dawkins, the owner/director of **Plane Designs**, wants you to produce an illustrated three-page, A4-sized, brochure that can be sent to potential customers to show what the company does.

Activities

The company, which is a member of the **Guild of Master Craftsmen**, has been in business for ten years next June and has a portfolio that includes:

- custom-made kitchens;   - suspended ceilings;

- making and fitting internal doors;   - a range of furniture;

- making and fitting French doors;   - making and fitting shelving;

- flooring;   - minor attic conversions.

The company has done work for private householders and businesses, both in the UK and in Sweden, France, Italy and Poland.

Your firm's address is - Timberwood House, Wood Lane, YOUR TOWN, GH5 3BC. Its telephone number is 01926 345123

1   Conduct some research into the work of joinery companies such as **Plane Designs** so you can describe what your firm does and include illustrations, perhaps of completed projects or objects of furniture, etc.

2   Put together your advertising brochure, the aim of which is to show your portfolio of past work and possible work and encourage custom. You might want to include illustrations of your workshop or some of the tools of the joinery trade, etc.

Task 27: Sunny Destinations Travel – A Customer Query

Student Information	Remember
In this task you will write a business letter replying to a customer's enquiry about flights to Belfast, and research information on Belfast and its attractions. Ask your tutor for a **Sunny Destinations Travel** letterheading.	Include your research documents with the task you hand to your tutor. It may be that you have to take a photocopy and attach this copy to your work. *See pages 76 - 83, Writing and Setting Out Business Letters.*

Conducting Research and Writing a Business Letter

Scenario

You have received a telephone message from a customer and have to reply to the questions asked.

Activities

1   Read the note of the telephone message – **Appendix 1**.

2   Use the details from the timetable – **Appendix 2** – to find the information the customer requires.

3   Conduct some research into the city of Belfast and its locality so you have information to include in the reply to the customer.

   A good starting point using the internet might be:
   www.discovernorthernireland.com

4   Write the letter of reply. You can sign the letter.

Overnight we've had a telephone message from Mr B Chalfont asking:

1 The times of the morning flights from the airport to Belfast.

2 He wants to go for 4 days so could you give him some information on the city - what to see, where it is located, etc. He also wants you to give him details of some places to stay and what the attractions are outside the city if he hires a car for two days.

His address is: Maple Cottage, The Green, Sethcote Village, YOUR TOWN YT23 3PC

Can you deal with this please?

Thank you

FLIGHTS FROM YOUR TOWN INTERNATIONAL AIRPORT

WEDNESDAY - 07:00 - 14:00

Destination	Departure Time	Flight Code
Belfast International	07:00	EV336
Nice	07:10	JB2281
Glasgow	07:20	EV662
Palma	07:45	GPL227
Valencia	07:50	SA229
Manchester	07:55	WW8837
Glasgow	08:10	WW6662
Belfast International	08:20	EV338
Newcastle	08:25	WW6771
Leeds-Bradford	08:30	JB2721
Nice	08:50	JB2283
Paris - CDG	09:00	AG771
Dublin	09:05	JB2416
Manchester	09:15	WW6801
Malaga	09:35	GPL239
Aberdeen	09:45	EV710
Belfast International	09:50	EV054
Newcastle	09:55	WW6673
Larnaca	10:15	EV887
Inverness	10:20	EV667
Amsterdam	10:40	WW3671
Plymouth	10:45	TT820
Barcelona	11:10	EV883
Malaga	11:25	GPL241
Wroclaw	11:45	JB8878
Pisa	12:00	TT902
Salzburg	12:15	EV330
Newcastle	12:25	FRD551
Prague	13:00	EV391
Faro	13:15	TT771
Bordeaux	13:20	WW3091
Cork	13:50	EV307
Dublin	13:55	JB2418
Paris- CDG	14:00	AG773

Task 28: Sethcote Stationery and Computing Supplies - A Customer Query

Student Information

In this task you will write a business letter replying to a customer's complaint. You will have to do some research before you can reply.

Ask your tutor for a **Sethcote Stationery and Computing Supplies** letterheading.

Remember

Include your research documents with the task you hand to your tutor. It may be that you have to take a photocopy and attach this copy to your work.

See pages 76 - 83, Writing and Setting Out Business Letters.

Conducting Research and Writing a Business Letter

Scenario

You work for **Sethcote Stationery and Computing Supplies** and the manager, Jeff Ainsworth, has passed to you a letter received today from a customer complaining about faulty goods bought in your store.

Jeff has asked you to reply to the customer.

Activities

1   Read the letter from the customer – **Appendix 1** – and Jeff's note on the bottom of it.

2   Carry out some research into the **Sale of Goods Act** to determine if the customer is right in asking for a refund, or alternatively what the store should do for him.

    Keep a copy of your research which will support what you put in your letter to the customer.

3   Write the letter to the customer. You will have to be polite, pointing out you are sorry he is having this problem, then say what we will do for him. Jeff Ainsworth will sign the letter.

Appendix 1

61 Pentland Grove
Chartworth Village
YOUR TOWN
HR6 7BW

Letter dated yesterday

The Manager
Sethcote Stationery and Computing Supplies
Sethcote House
Bamfield Way
YOUR TOWN
YW3 5BK

Dear Sir or Madam

My recent purchase of a KB Fast Feed 772 Colour Laser Printer

I purchased a laser printer from your store on 30th (last month), so this piece of equipment is less than one month old. Although I have successfully installed the printer, and it does print, it only prints one page of any document, then crumples the following pages until they get stuck and I have to take off the front cover and clear the paper jam. At that point, when I resend the document, it again prints only one page then the error is repeated.

Clearly the printer is not of satisfactory quality and neither is it fit for purpose. Accordingly I intend to bring the printer back to your store on Saturday for a refund. I want you to know I am aware of my rights under consumer law and I do not intend to accept an exchange or to have this printer repaired.

I shall be in the store at around 10 am so I shall expect to see you then.

Yours faithfully

Colin Random

Colin Random

I'm not sure about this. My reaction is to offer him a replacement printer ot a credit note - I don't see why he should have a refund.

I want to write to him to explain what we will do on Saturday so could you find out about this for me, please then write the letter for me to sign.

Thank you

Jeff

Task 29: First Steps to Fitness – The Benefits of Exercise

Student Information	Remember
In this task you will research a fitness regime and make a short presentation. You might want to ask your tutor for the **First Steps to Fitness** logo document.	Include your research documents with the task you hand to your tutor. It may be that you have to take a photocopy and attach this copy to your work. *See pages 106 - 110, Taking Part in a Discussion and Making a Presentation.*

Conducting Research and Making a Presentation

Scenario

You work for **First Steps to Fitness** in the marketing department and have to research certain aspects of fitness regimes and make a presentation to the instructors and the marketing manager so they can decide which classes to add to their existing timetable.

Activities

Appendix 1 contains some details of the "Spinning" exercise regime, which gives ideas about the type of information you might like to include in your work. It describes the sport, its benefits, and gives some ideas of the range of classes offered.

You must produce a similar sheet – which will form the basis of your presentation – on **two** from the following regimes:

- Tai Chi
- Kick Boxing
- Aqua Aerobics
- Pilates
- Salsa
- Yoga

1. Carry out research into your two chosen areas, looking for information to describe the regime, its benefits, the levels (if appropriate), and a contact name and number.

2. Put together a presentation that will last **no fewer than four minutes** and **no longer than six minutes**. The purpose is to **inform** the audience about your chosen areas of fitness to **encourage** them to introduce classes to the health club.

   Your presentation will include a handout on each area chosen, similar to the one shown in **Appendix 1**, but including an appropriate image.

3. Make your presentation and be prepared to answer questions from your audience.

FIRST STEPS TO FITNESS

Health Club
www.fstf.health.com
01533 670082

Spinning sets your heart racing

What is Spinning?

Aerobics on bikes that don't move.

Using the tempo of the music, the pace is varied throughout the session. Each bike is individually set up for the person using it, so people of any fitness level can take part in the same class.

Benefits

Spinning improves your general fitness, tones muscles and is a great way to burn calories.

Type of Classes Offered

Spin for Beginners: Session lasts 45 minutes.

Learn the techniques in this introductory class then progress to the next level.

Spin, spin and spin again: Session lasts 35 minutes

A way to unwind. This class offers a lighter approach and is a good way to unwind after a hard day at work.

For details of all spinning classes contact Bradley on 01533 670117

Task 30: Primary Colours - Paint Sales

Student Information	Remember
In this task you will interpret graphs and write a report.	Present your findings in a logical and clear way, making use of paragraph headings, underlined text, columns of text, etc., so that the reader can understand, at a glance, what you write. *See pages 92 - 97, Writing Reports.*

Interpreting Graphs and Writing a Report

Scenario

You work in **Primary Colours** and one of the partners, Peter Campion, has asked you to prepare a report to reflect paint sales in the last quarter.

Activities

1   The graphs shown in **Appendix 1** show the sales of "Soft Sheen Emulsion" paint for the last quarter (the three months before this month). You have to prepare a suitably worded report for Peter Campion that gives the following details:

Title: Soft Sheen Emulsion Paint Sales (in litres) *then add the months and year.*

Report for: Mr Peter Campion, Partner.

Date of report: *Today's date*

Findings:

then under this heading display, **for each of the colours (in each graph)**, the name of the paint colour that sold **best** and the name of the paint colour that sold the **least well**. Support your findings with figures.

Recommendations:

   a)   You will recommend the withdrawal of the paint colours that sold the fewest litres;

   b)   You will recommend an advertising campaign for any paint that sold fewer than 2000 litres (name the colours).

Sign the report.

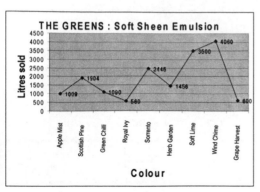

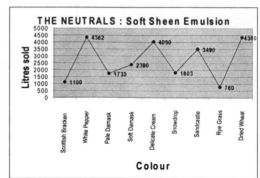

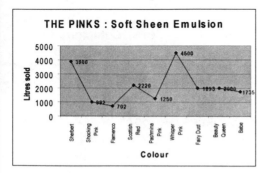

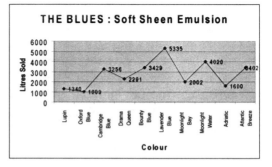

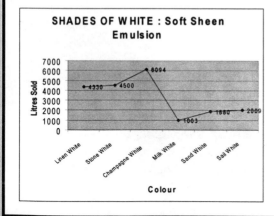

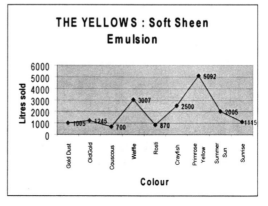

Task 31: Personal Interest – Applying for a Job and Attending an Interview

Student Information	Remember
In this task you will locate a job for which to apply, write a CV and covering letter and be interviewed for the post.	*See pages 99 - 103, Writing a CV and a Covering Letter.* *See pages 104 and 105, Interview Tips.*

Applying for a Job and Attending an Interview

Scenario

As you approach the end of your studies you will probably be looking for employment, even if it is only part-time until the next part of your education begins.

In this task you will be locating a job for which you want to apply, writing a CV and covering letter and then you will be interviewed for the position.

Activities

1 Locate an advertisement for a job in which you are interested. If possible take a photocopy of this job description, or alternatively, write down its details.

2 Put together a CV which is appropriately worded.

3 Prepare a covering letter to accompany the CV and make sure it contains information relevant to the job.

4 You have been called for an interview (your tutor(s) will interview you). Prepare some questions you will ask and think about your answers to the questions the interviewers might ask you.

5 Attend the interview, after which you will be told whether or not you have got the job.

Good luck.

Task 32: General Interest - Fair Trade

Student Information	Remember
In this task you will research information, put together a fact sheet and make a presentation of one aspect of your findings on the topic.	*See pages 106 - 110, Taking Part in a Discussion and Making a Presentation.*

Conducting Research and Making a Presentation

Scenario

You have heard a little about **The Fairtrade Foundation** and want to find out what it is and what the organisation does.

You will conduct some research and make a presentation to group members. Assume the **audience** knows little, if nothing, about the Foundation.

Activities

1   Conduct some research into the topic. Your first approach might be to visit the organisation's web site, www.fairtrade.org.uk. You will find information from other sources **and include all your research documents when you hand in this task**.

From your research you need sufficient information to complete the following tasks:

a)   write a **fact sheet** the **purpose** of which is to educate readers about the Foundation, what it does and why it is important, and

b)   produce a **handout** for the audience to whom you make a presentation on **one** aspect of the topic.

You need to find out such things as:

- what Fairtrade is all about (who they are, what they do, etc.);
- any facts and figures of interest;
- which products are included in the Fairtrade categories;
- the benefits to Fairtrade members;
- which countries are represented in the Fairtrade Foundation;

and anything else you consider relevant and interesting.

2   Prepare your **fact sheet**, and consider including illustrations to emphasise your points and to help the reader better understand the topic.

3   Select one, possibly two, areas from your research and prepare presentation notes and a handout for your audience. The **purpose** of the handout is to help them to understand the topic, or perhaps test their knowledge at the end of your talk - to see if they have been listening!!

4   Make your presentation, which must last **no longer than five minutes**, and prepare for questions afterwards.

Task 33: General Interest - Blue Flag Beaches in the United Kingdom

Student Information	Remember
In this task you will research information, put together a fact sheet and make a presentation of one aspect of your findings on the topic.	*See pages 106 - 110, Taking Part in a Discussion and Making a Presentation.*

Conducting Research and Making a Presentation

Scenario

Friends of yours are planning to take a beach holiday in the UK this year and you have been asked to carry out some research for them.

You will conduct some research and make a presentation to group members. It is clear the **audience** knows little, if anything, about the topic.

Activities

1   Conduct some research into the topic. Your first approach might be to visit the web site www.blueflag.org.uk. You will find information from other sources **and include all your research documents when you hand in this task.**

From your research you need sufficient information to complete the following tasks:

   a)   write a **fact sheet** the **purpose** of which is to educate readers about the topic; and

b)   produce a **handout** for your audience to whom you will make a presentation on **one** aspect of the topic.

You need to find out such things as:

- what the Blue Flag organisation is;
- what its criteria are for awarding a beach a Blue Flag;
- the Blue Flag beaches in different parts of the country to where you live (as your friends will not wish to holiday in their area);
- specific details of one or two beaches from your list;
- the criteria the organisation uses when deciding water is safe and healthy;
- what is the 'Waterside Code';

and anything else you consider relevant and interesting.

2   Prepare your **fact sheet**, and consider including illustrations to emphasise your points and to help the reader better understand the topic.

3   Select one, possibly two, areas from your research and prepare presentation notes and a handout for your audience. The **purpose** of the handout is to help them to understand the topic, or perhaps test their knowledge at the end of your talk - to see if they have been listening!!

4   Make your presentation, which must last **no longer than five minutes**, and prepare for questions afterwards.

Photo by Emily Kench

Solutions to Exercises for Section 1

Page 6

1 We're
2 It's
3 They're
4 isn't
5 I'm
6 It's   haven't
7 What's
8 It's   they're
9 You're   aren't
10 it'll   I've

Page 10

1 the boy's hat
2 the chair's legs
3 the man's briefcase
4 the dog's bone
5 the student's pen

Page 13

1 the clubs' football ground
2 the students' text books
3 the tutors' pens
4 the cars' exhausts
5 the boxers' competitions

Page 14

1 The children's playground
2 The school's piano
3 The piano's keys
4 The cats' whiskers
5 The gentlemen's club
6 The policemen's uniforms
7 The student's computer
8 The man's car
9 The car's steering wheel
10 The employee's desk

Page 15

1 achieve
2 believe
3 ceiling
4 freight
5 neighbours
6 piece
7 priest
8 receipt
9 reign
10 relief
11 sleigh
12 veins
13 weigh
14 yield

Page 16

```
M A L M H E O S D F G Q O R A
U K O Z F P B T N W L X D C E
R E L I E F H G I E W D H G V
U T E P V I M O N E T I N H E
S R U O B H G I E N E I G V I
T P R T Z S B A A V L I S V L
X S I H P I S J E I E T E D E
S L E E D I X V E L H I L G B
L C H I C E E C S G N E L E A
L J I X R E Y C I S I U R G W
A C Z C Q P Q E E Y M J J X N
C E Y M D L R E S R Z V S K D
U V I U V F U N G I E R H R X
S I F T D Q X X D H Z T M U H
V J Z L K U K E I C S Z A R F
```

Page 18

1 there
2 there
3 Their   they're
4 there
5 They're   their   there
6 They're
7 They're
8 their
9 There   their
10 Their   there

Page 21

1 too
2 too
3 two
4 to
5 to two
6 too to
7 to two
8 too
9 to to
10 two too

Page 23

1 where
2 Where
3 were
4 we're
5 were
6 Where
7 we're
8 where
9 we're
10 were

Page 25

1 here
2 hear

3 here
4 here
5 here
6 heard
7 hear
8 here   hear
9 here
10 here

Page 27

1 number
2 number
3 amount
4 number
5 amount
6 number
7 amount
8 amount
9 number
10 amount

Page 29

1 less
2 fewer
3 fewer
4 less
5 less
6 fewer
7 fewer
8 less
9 fewer
10 fewer

Page 31

1 accept
2 accept
3 except
4 accept
5 except

6 accept

7 accept

8 except

9 accept

10 except

Page 33

1 advise

2 advice

3 advise

4 advice

5 advice

6 advice

7 advice

8 advice

9 advise

10 advice

Page 35

1 practise

2 practise

3 practice

4 practice

5 practice

6 practise

7 practise

8 practice

9 practise

10 practice

Page 37

1 affect

2 affect

3 affect

4 effect

5 effect

6 affect

7 affect

8 effect

9 affect

10 effect

Page 39

1 borrow

2 lends

3 borrow

4 lend

5 lend

6 borrow

7 lend

8 borrowed

9 lend

10 borrow

Page 42

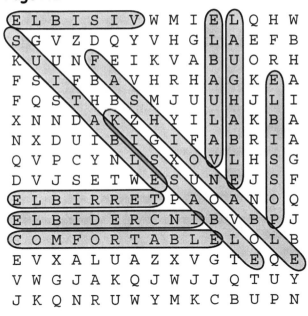

Page 47

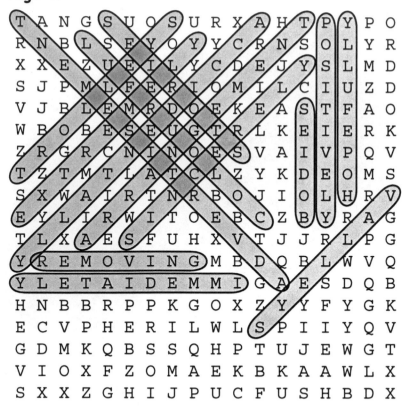

Page 51

1 **sat** in the garden
2 **will** work.
3 **will** have to buy a new one.
4 everyone **was** thinking England **would** lose.
5 will **have seen**   **closes** next week.
6 **are** going to Brussels
7 which **are** lovely to see.
8 **is** likely to succeed.
9 **are** trying
10 he **took**

Lightning Source UK Ltd.
Milton Keynes UK
20 June 2010

155798UK00001B/89/P